Rivers Running Far

Also by the same author :

Roots of Stone

Rivers Running Far

The Story of Those Who Went Away

Hugh Allison

Librario

Published by

Librario Publishing Ltd.

ISBN No: 1-904440-70-3

Copies can be ordered from retail
or via the internet at:
www.librario.com

or from:

Brough House
Milton Brodie
Kinloss
Moray
IV36 2UA
Tel / Fax: 01343 850617

Printed in Times.

Cover design and layout by Steven James
www.chimeracreations.co.uk

Printed and bound by
DigiSource (GB) Ltd.

Dedication

Annan, Tweed and Clyde
Rise a' oot o' ae hillside;
Tweed ran, Annan wan,
Clyde fell, and brak its neck owre Corra Linn.

The old couplet which describes, rightly or wrongly, the rising of three famous rivers from the one source area is rarely truer than when applied to the people of Scotland.

When I think of my father's people in Scotland, and in Australia, and in America, I am reminded that the same hillside was the source for all.

This book is dedicated to my father, whose heart is shared in equal measure, between the Highlands, of which he has become part, and his Clydesdale, which nurtured him as he grew.

It is a" thank you" for the many times that he took me tramping in the hills and glens of both areas, and for the gifts of the tales and stories that he related as we travelled.

It was during these rambles that he imparted the principles of fairness and equality, and the concept of the world as home and family, worthy of attention and respect.

"For a' that and a' that
It's comin yet for a' that,
That man to man the world o'er
Shall brithers be for a' that."
Robert Burns

Contents

Maps

Tables

Illustrations

Acknowledgements

This book, *Rivers Running Far* has its origins in my earlier work, *Roots of Stone*. In a spirit of balance, it seemed to me that after focusing a light on the forebears of one ancestral branch, something similar should be attempted for the other branch. Once that idea had arisen, it was closely followed by a question. What story is waiting to be added to the Book of All Tales?

Emigration was an issue touched on towards the end of *Roots of Stone*, and, given the image I had carried since youth, of my father's people flowing out from Scotland across the world, it seemed like it should be the central thread to the story waiting to be told. The Story of those who went away!

Working on *Rivers Running Far* has enriched my life beyond any of the expectations I may previously have entertained. It is a book which required much research, which, in turn, led to me working with many remarkable and uplifting people. Some of these I have known since birth, while others are more recent acquaintances. They brought an energy and sense of excitement to this project of mine, and the help and assistance of so many willing and enthusiastic individuals has significantly lightened the burden of that research, and added the element of fun.

Writing this book has created the opportunity to get to know relatives from three different continents, who up until this time were only known by me as names on charts. Another unforeseen outcome was in being able to enjoy the truly warm and welcoming hospitality of these family members, in the United States of America and in Australia.

I must also endorse the discovery which I spoke of, in *Roots of Stone*, that the Glasgow maxim of 'one singer, one song' doesn't hold in the world of writing. There are parts of the lives of many people contained within these pages. Anecdotes and information have been tendered willingly in anticipation of the finished story. This help and material, from people here and abroad kept me encouraged and productive. It also created a welcome obligation upon me to ensure that I finished the work.

I would like to thank my wife for her belief in the relevance of the work, and my father for his patience with some of my more inane questions. He has coped with great diplomacy during the many visits in which I questioned him about some detail, or other, with regard to early family life. I was very gratified one day, however, when my mother remarked how our conversations resembled those that took place in times past, between older and younger members of a household. It was the old way of learning about one's own individual heritage. That type of family interaction has, in part, become a casualty of the modern lifestyle, and it's gradual disappearance is another good reason to add this story to the Book of All Tales.

Thanks also to Dougie at Nairn Post Office, and Calum Grant, for their help, and to Robert Walker in Wales, for his knowledge. The staff at Culloden Battlefield have shown continuing patience with my excitements, and Liz Fischer, Ed Ingle, and Luke & Meredith McCahan were all hugely helpful during my trip to the United States.

My deepest appreciation, as before, is reserved for the long-suffering small band of heroes who helped me throughout, reading and patiently rereading, as I would tinker with nuance and issues of clarity, etc:

Scotland
David, Mary, Lindsay, Kerry and Dawn Allison, and Duncan Cook.

America
Both John Doerrs, Lynn Shelton, Kathy Williams, Venessa MacIntosh, the Morrow Allisons, Norma Allison, and Arne Trelvik.

Australia
Reg, Judith, George, Libby, Jim, Thelma, Alan, Anthea, Adele and Mark Minto, Jane Shannon, Elizabeth Dodd, Joan Heilbronn, and Alison Stasa.

Acknowledgements

Professional
Thanks to The National Archives of Scotland, the Mitchell Library, Townsville Maritime Museum, the Australian National Archives in Brisbane and Canberra, Warren County Museum in Lebanon, Ohio, and the Salem Township Public Library in Morrow, who all helped to keep an amateur like me on track and accurate.

Further, very specific thanks are due to authors of those works from which I have taken short quotes to help underline or clarify portions of the narrative:

Professor Ted Cowan, Montrose: *For Covenant and King* (page 34)
HMSO, *Patent 2670* (page 90)
The National Archives of Scotland, *ex AF 51/17* (page 123)
AF 51/90 (page 127)
GD 248/702/5/56 (page 130)
Professor T C Smout, *A Century of the Scottish People*
1830 – 1950 (page 130 – 131)
James Boswell, *Journal of a Tour to the Hebrides* (page 126)
Tom Steel, *Scotland's Story* (page 140)
Geoffrey Blainey, *Black Kettle and Full Moon* (page 156)
Margaret and Alastair Macfarlane, *The Scottish Radicals*
(page 159)
Celeste Ray, *Highland Heritage* (pages 192, 193, 204 and 205)

Robert and Maggie at Hi-Arts were supportive and helpful, and finally, in closing, I am grateful to those at Librario Publishing. They made the final stages of this literary journey as exciting as the early days. Thank you.

Thanks are also due to the Scottish Arts Council, and Highlands and Islands Enterprise, for part-funding the American research costs.

Introduction

This book, *Rivers Running Far*, is the story of those who went away. In other words it's an exploration of the emigration of the Scots to various places across the world. The principal destinations around which the tales are spun are Australia and the United States of America.

The diaspora of the Scots is a phenomenon which touches the lives of tens of millions of people worldwide. This book contains more questions than answers. This, however, is part of its universal relevance. The set of factors leading to emigration were different in every case, as were the outcomes of the decision to leave. There is no single conclusion, and so the author, instead, seeks to identify general trends, and the questions with which anyone could begin to investigate their own forebears' motivations.

The aim of this work is broad, combining findings from scholarly and archival sources with the varied real life experiences of many individuals from a number of different ancestry streams. In timeline the story ranges from the Stone Age through to the present day, and the reader finds the action coming at them from four different continents.

The Prologue opens on a misty morning in Lanark. The tale begins with a stranger walking by, and the reader follows. As the mist dissipates, so does the mystery surrounding the stranger, and the words begin to describe the very axle around which this whole narrative work revolves.

Later, a brief emigration by the author's parents in mid 20th century is the introduction to questions like why and where people go, what they experience, and how it changes them. The prologue closes with a reminder that emigrants and Scots expatriots are ever in our minds, and a welcome awaits them.

Chapter One describes a journey anti-clockwise around Tinto Hill, in Lanarkshire. This is where one branch of the author's ancestors, the Mintos, are first found, and their lives from 1760 to 1890 are described in these pages.

As the reader circles Tinto, they travel ever farther back in time, and hear tales of Covenanters and Royalists, William Wallace and Marian Braidfoot, Iron Age Forts, Bronze Age Cairns, and Stone Age Hunters. This land has been settled for millennia, and asking the question "why do people stay" can often be as productive as asking the question "why do they go". The chapter ends by introducing the concept that people move on because of a force, and that this force can be internal desire or external duress.

The second chapter is set in the ancestral Allison lands of the lower Clyde Basin, (around Paisley and Erskine). After a peaceful opening sequence in the Iron Age things soon get shaken up by Agricola's Roman invasion. The words attributed to Calgacus at the Battle of Mons Graupius are recorded here, and reappear later too. After the Romans leave it isn't long until the Viking threat arises. This leads to a uniting of the realm by around the 9th Century.

Monks and Warriors, Farmers and Tradesmen all pass before the reader as time races by. William Wallace shows up in Elderslie in the 13th Century, and ultimately, the Allisons appear, as Farmers, in 1711. They successfully weather the Jacobite Risings, and we follow several generations until 1792. In conclusion, the author compares and considers the principles enshrined in three very significant historical documents – Calgacus' address, The Declaration of Arbroath, and The Declaration of American Independence.

Chapters Three and Four cover the Georgian, Victorian and Edwardian eras, or to be more exact, 1747 – 1921. Within these years Scotland was subject to huge change. This was the time of the agricultural improvers, the industrial revolution, and the Age of Enlightenment. Following the Napoleonic War, it was also the period characterised by the Radical Wars and the Chartist movement. The reader is introduced to whole new generations of Mintos and Allisons, all living within the strictures of their place and time. Some of them are seen to be making decisions about whether or not to join the popular move towards emigration. Others are content with their place.

The early part of the twentieth century is characterised by political unrest, and the names Keir Hardie, John MacLean and "Red Clydeside" are frequently heard.

The international situation in Europe becomes ever more tense, throughout the early years of the twentieth century. Yet the young Minto girls, Ruth and Mary, seem not to notice, deciding therefore to take a holiday in France at the end of July 1914. Hence much of Chapter Four is the unpublished diary of Ruth, a young Scots girl trapped in France at the outbreak of the Great War.

Many Mintos are lost in the conflict, but not Ruth. Alexander Allison, despite a very active war, also survives, and as the light fades, on Chapter Four, we see these two becoming married, thus binding the families together.

Chapter Five is the story of George and Agnes Minto, and their five sons, who emigrated to Queensland, Australia in 1911. As George was a master- blacksmith, the reader is treated to tales of smiths and smithing, as well as family anecdotes. The story of "the patent" emerges, as do the difficulties that the dawn of the age of the motor car brings. Finally the Mintos choose to emigrate, and travel on the Otway, narrowly avoiding nautical tragedy. They settle down to live in Brisbane, but it is only a few short years until George is killed in World War I, leaving Agnes widowed with five boys on an unfamiliar continent.

America was John Allison's continent of choice, though given his desertion from the British army in the mid-nineteenth century, it was perhaps more necessity than preference. Chapter Six describes how he entered the United States by the Canada Route and was soon embroiled in the American Civil War. After heroic service, he settled near Cincinnati. Other Allisons soon followed, including, rather confusingly, his nephew, who was also called John. This nephew was soon to become a sharp-shooting Sheriff undertaker! His uncle John was finally pardoned by the war office and permitted to visit Scotland around 1910. Then the shadow of World War I fell. But when it lifted, old John still had all his boys, and by 1921 was celebrating his 90th birthday.

Chapter Seven looks in context at everything the reader has learned about emigration in the course of the narrative. By use of many sources and actual examples, the concept of external and internal forces is revisited. The nature/nurture debate is explained, and the patterns that govern choice of destination are examined. There is also a definition of culture, together with some thoughts regarding the part that it plays in the emigration game.

The next three chapters move from the early years of the twentieth century, and the Great Depression, through World War Two, and into the modern era. These common threads are woven throughout each of the chapters, as Scotland, Australia, and America are looked at in turn.

Chapter Eight opens with the return of the Scottish troops from the Great War. Politics and revolution are in the air, and Lloyd George's promises of "a land fit for heroes" are beginning to sound hollow. Returning hero, Alexander Allison, and Ruth, his bride, were luckier than some. In 1921 they became the first tenants of one of the earliest council houses to be built in Scotland. This was at the beginning of The Roaring Twenties, a decade of contradictions. The liberality and extravagance of the privileged couldn't hide the bread-lines, unemployment and despair of the poor. As the century wore on, the next generation of Allisons had to cope with the tragic early loss of a parent, and then the onset of World War Two. Both children followed medical careers, and the years and generations run on, down to the author, pen in hand.

Chapter Nine covers the same period, but uses the five sons of George Minto, to help lift the cover off Australia's tales of the twentieth century. There are hard stories of the depression years, and of mining jobs in remote areas. There are sea stories, such as "The search for the Kobenhavn", a sailing ship lost in the southern ocean. War stories include tales of Burma, Mediterranean convoys, and "The truth behind the Darwin Raid" – which was a bigger offensive than Pearl Harbour. George's great-great grandchildren even manage to make a brief appearance, towards the end of the chapter.

Chapter Ten completes this trilogy of chapters, looking, as it does, at the descendants of "Old John", and Sheriff John. It charts the beginnings of the "Allison and Rose" alliance, and then the onset of the Great Depression. Sheriff John's daughter Bessie tackled the Depression head-on, ensuring that many people retained both jobs and homes. In the war years, she offered sanctuary to her Scottish relatives. 1944 also saw the tragic and early death of young Johnnie Allison in Morrow. The chapter concludes with mention of the Allison Tartan, and a proposal for it's future distribution in America.

Chapter Eleven is similar in type to Chapter Seven, in that it reviews the story so far, and uses tales that have cropped up in the narrative to best illustrate particular threads. It considers specifically the areas of heritage and tradition, the fragility of family knowledge, and instances of the mysterious, the co-incidental, and the inexplicable. It concludes with a look at the importance of both people and places, in the creation of heritage.

The Epilogue to this whole book of tales asks questions about the importance of genealogy in today's society, and the "pros" and "cons" in having such knowledge of one's ancestors. The changing place of ancestral tourism through the years of the twentieth century is investigated, as is the idea of universal brotherhood /sisterhood.

This tale of Rivers Running Far concludes with a thought or two on the stubborn nature of the Scot, refusing to consider separation as having permanence.

Early Mist

*"The sublime horrors of
this majestic scene"*
Thomas Newte

Mist lies across fields of Clydesdale, unmoving in the early morning still. The overall effect is of an underwater world of ghostly trees on the field boundaries, and a strangely muffled reality. The sun is just beginning to light the sky as it climbs above the Southern Uplands, and the light is weak and diffuse. Footfalls sound, and a figure appears on Hyndford Road. The mist frays, all unwilling, to allow passage, and closes in again, behind the young man, as he turns down towards Robiesland.

Later, when this early shroud has worn away into strips and tatters, we wonder where he might have gone. So we follow. Down past the stately trees of Bonnington Parkland and out into the green fields. Here, the last vestiges of mist can be seen, ahead and to the left, filling the depths of a great cleft in the earth.

Above this wooded valley, high on its northern shoulder, stands a curious structure, as testimony both to the awesome grandeur of this place, and the ingenuity of some of those folks who came before. This is the Mirror House, built in 1708. The mirrors in the back wall gave the visitor the illusion that they were standing right below one of the most spectacular sights of Scotland, while those less troubled by vertigo could stand out on the lookout and view directly the "sublime horrors of this majestic scene".

Our young man is here, standing on the lookout, and waiting for the last of the mist to shred and disperse. When it does, the magnificent sight of

Corra Linn is the awaited reward. Tradition tells that this waterfall, where the Clyde plunges a total of 90 feet, is named for the mythical Caledonian princess, Cora, who is said to have leapt, on horseback, from the cliff into the river.

As the greatest of the Falls of Clyde, this is one of the places that fired the imaginations of writers and painters of the "Romantic" period. The Wordsworths described the vista. Several artists, including Turner, painted the Falls. Is this perhaps our young man. Or could he be one of the other enthusiastic visitors to have trod upon this lookout – Coleridge, or Sir Walter Scott.

Then again, the early morning mist may have misled. This is not, after all, the beginning of the nineteenth century. This is the very midst of the twentieth century.

Two world wars are now left behind, and maybe, just maybe, a period of prosperity beckons. It could be a good time to make plans for the future. Is this what the young man muses upon.

A smile hovers at his lips, and his eyes crinkle, at the thought of that nonsense about "Lord Minto of Tinto". She hadn't believed for a moment that he held such a title, but it had been fun to pretend. And it did make a good story, given both his middle name, and his fondness for Tinto Hill. The pleasing daftness of it was just one more example of the effect that this girl from the far north had on him.

And so David Allison moved another step closer to that decision to share his life with Margaret Macdonald from Sutherland. They were both medical students in Glasgow and had met in his fourth year, in 1946, as she began doing hospital clinics.

Shared coffees, and shared interests brought them closer, at a time when the world was reshaping itself from the wreckage of war. Out from under the shadow of that conflict, the air seemed somehow clearer and more full of possibilities. There was suddenly time for fun, and time too for planning. Thus 1947 was the time, and a misty Lanark morning the place, when David began thinking of settling down.

Duty and distance are very effective barriers to romance, especially when, (within a few scant months), Glasgow was half a world away. That part of his life was temporarily on hold.

University of Glasgow.

When the sun rose, it leapt into the sky. The early morning colours were vivid. There was no slow-time between night and day. This was a country untouched by gentle Scottish mists, and the weak, diffuse morning light of northern climes. In fact, there was nothing diffident about this country at all.

Everything had an immediacy, from the heavy smell of the heat and dust of the bush country, through the feel of a faraway soil underfoot, to some of the insistent chatter of the locals. "Effendi", they called him. He knew that it meant "Someone of rank", but as yet he hadn't made much further inroads into the Somali language. It wasn't one he'd learned before coming, because, after all, he hadn't been planning on coming here. He'd been destined for Kenya, hence his learning of Swahili. He had in fact been in Kenya – but only for a few weeks, before getting the instruction to move on. And so here he was, Lt David Allison, Royal Army Medical Corps, in Italian Somaliland, admiring the African sunrise, nursing a black eye, and wondering if it was time to send a letter back to his fiancée, Margaret, in Scotland.

In hindsight he was glad that he had become engaged before being sent to this far corner of the globe. It was now 1948, and this was National Service – the requirement to give two years service in a branch of the armed forces. And so he had found himself in Somaliland, by way of Aldershot, the Suez Canal Zone, and that brief period in Kenya.

Next steps, beyond getting a greater grip of the language, included the effective medical administration of the Upper Juba Province. This included the hospital in Iscia Baidoa and a hinterland of mixed jungle, river and miles of dense bush over an area larger in size than Wales. And over and above that, treating his black eye.

What black eye? One of the year's sporting highlights was the cricket match between the Kings African Rifles, and the Civil Authorities, for whom David played. These "Civils" enjoyed socialising with their Ethiopian counterparts from over the border. Not surprisingly, they were all to be found in the bar, the night before the match. Unfortunately, so were the opposition – a number of British NCO's from the King's African Rifles. And worse, these were the kind of military colonialists who took exception to mixing with the locals. Seeing the Civils drinking with the Ethiopians was therefore the spark that lit their fuse. Before long there was a different kind of match in progress – that much older sport, the bar-room brawl.

The next day's cricket was somewhat embarrassing, with people in both teams taking the field in a variety of dark glasses. David, on stepping up, as eleventh man, proved that upholding people's rights by night doesn't necessarily make you a good cricketer by day. He swung his bat to give the ball a mighty swipe, and promptly knocked his own bails off.

Many more East African adventures were to follow, and if this work were to be a journal of David Allison's time in Africa then they would be included here. I hope that someday soon he may be persuaded to put pen to paper and create just such a record. But for now, that is not the story contained in these pages, and time is running on, like sand through the hourglass.

The world turns, the African sun rises and falls, and eventually our eager young man boards ship in Mogadishu, and sails for home. He makes landfall in time for Christmas 1949, and is married to Margaret, from Sutherland, the following year. Their first home is in Clarkston in Glasgow, and it is here that the first of their children is born. This is Alastair, and within a couple of years he is joined by a sister, Anne, although by this time the family is living in Dumbarton.

And this next is the very axle around which this whole narrative work revolves. Although they were settled, in employment, and culturally well-nested, (at the foot of the rock that was an early Capital in Scotland), they left. Not just Dumbarton, but, in fact, the whole country. Within a year or so of Anne's birth they had emigrated, like so many others had, before them. This, then, stimulates all the questions in my mind about why it is that people choose to go? Where they go? What they experience? and how it changes them?

However, perhaps unusually, within a year this particular family, my family, were back in Scotland, thus drawing out a different set of questions – What hadn't worked? What pulled them back? Why did they return, while some others never did? How did they feel to be back?

My father, very recently, supplied the answers to these questions for me, and so launched me on the road to investigating the motives and imperatives behind the other emigrations within the family. With David and Margaret, the weight that started the emigration process was a desire for betterment for the family. By 1953 they had been in Dumbarton for three years, David working as an assistant GP.

The prospect an assistant GP nowadays is to achieve full partnership within months. Back then, however, this was not the case.

Sometimes many years could pass. Almost 3 years had slipped by, in Dumbarton, when the door-bell rang. All unlooked for, a member of a well known Lanark family had come seeking David. This man had gone to considerable trouble to find the address, and came with an opportunity. As senior partner in a Kent-based medical practice, he was offering a good package, both financially, and in terms, together with prospects of a partnership after one year. It was the word "prospects" that did it. With four futures to provide for, suddenly Ashford in Kent started to look good. On checking with the current senior partner in Dumbarton it seemed that there was no chance for an early partnership there.

So they packed up the Austin 12 and headed for southern England. Life in Ashford was fine, but as the year was wearing on, decision-time loomed ever closer. Fine is fine, but it isn't necessarily right. There were cultural and social differences. The south-east of England has a strong Norman legacy, and feudal times live on even today, enshrined in the very stratified society and class system endemic in those parts of Britain. Scotland is, in general, very egalitarian, - (a man's a man for a' that) – and the adjustment that was required of them just proved too great. The other factor that led to the return to Scotland was the desire to provide the children with the best start in life. It seemed that a Scottish education – (at that time the envy of the world) – was the way to do it.

June 1954 saw them packing up the Austin 12 again, and heading back to Scotland, this time to an assistant GP's job in Lochaber. It was a good call, because by 1957 there was a full partnership, and two more boys, William and Hugh, appeared in 1955 and 1960 respectively.

Mist lies across fields of Clydesdale, unmoving in the early morning still. The overall effect is of an underwater world of ghostly trees on the field boundaries, and a strangely muffled reality. The sun is just beginning to light the sky as it climbs above the Southern Uplands, and the light is weak and diffuse. Footfalls sound, and two figures appear on Hyndford Road. The mist frays, all unwilling, to allow passage, and closes in again, behind the man and the boy, as they turn in, towards Lanark Loch.

They'd been walking, as I should know. I was the smaller figure. And during the walk came the talk. My father, David Allison, was a busy man, and so times such as these were like uncovered gold. Furthermore, like buried treasure, each piece was worthy of careful consideration.

What he told me on this day stayed with me always. He spoke of the streams of emigrants from Scotland, and of the people from our own family that had gone out to faraway places, all across the world, and as I thought of it, inside my head I saw them as rivers, running far.

The home-place is always present in the heart, no matter the separation of time and distance. I presume that this is felt keenly by all, but I know for sure that it is felt keenly by Scots. I have felt the feather edge of that steel wire myself, when working overseas. I hope, therefore, that this work, "Rivers Running Far" will speak to Scots expatriots and emigrants everywhere, and remind them that they are ever in our minds, and a welcome awaits them.

"The door is open, and the kettle is on. Come away in!"

Scotland Today.

Chapter One

Flying on Tinto

"On Tintock tap there is a mist,
And in the mist there is a kist,
And in the kist there is a caup,
And in the caup there is a drap;
Tak' up the caup, drink aff the drap,
And set the caup on Tintock Tap."
Anon

Tinto, a southern giant, stately in her isolation, dominates Lanark's southern horizon. At 2,320 feet, this hill is a modern magnet for hang-gliders, microlights, and para-gliders. The great dome of red Felsite rocks provide the ideal launch spot from which to take to the skies over southern and central Scotland. As the thermals provide lift, and ever greater heights are achieved, then the views widen in all directions.

The Lowther Hills stand to the south, and Culter Fell to the east, while to the north lies the whole Midland valley – Forth to Clyde – with the jagged blue shield-wall of the Highlands rising in the distance beyond. Far to the west the valleys run down into Ayrshire – the Earldom of Carrick, of Robert the Bruce's time. The names thereabouts have a romance and fire that brings to mind the martial past. Both Wallace and Bruce won great victories at Loudon Hill, against the English forces of occupation. Still later, in 1679, a large covenanting force defeated Claverhouse and the Royalists, at the Battle of Drumclog.

Tinto's own name, too, recalls a long ago past. It is thought that the name is from the time, centuries gone, when the height was used as a beacon hill. It seems likely that it derives from the Gaelic word "Teinteach", meaning fiery, and thus it shares such a history with summits like Ben Lomond and others.

This peak, so bold amidst the surrounding countryside, has also, long, been a centre for human settlement. Walking the slopes can be a little like a journey through history. If we take a stroll widdershins, (anti-clockwise), around the hill, then we get the chance to visit a number of sites, each of which will take us progressively farther back through time, in this land where the first of the Mintos are recorded as living and working.

Tinto Hill.

The old Great Western Road from Glasgow to England used to climb over Tinto's western flank. The journey took the traveller through the aptly named "Howgate Mouth". A writer and statist of 1791 described this journey as being "little more than seven feet wide, the mountain rising steep on each side". Transport changes around 1800 led to the need for improved roads. The Howgate route proved too steep and hazardous for some of the new coaches, and so was superseded by the new Carlisle Turnpike. The new road was designed by Thomas Telford, and involved laying a raft of brushwood over the marshy Thankerton Moor. This formed the base for the new toll road, (or Carlisle Turnpike), and is still the route of the A73 to this day.

The Howgate mouth road twists torturously through its narrow pass, and then bends swiftly down onto the Wiston-Rigside Road, at Sornfallow. This farm was tilled and turned by generations of the Plenderleith family. It lies in a wooded fold of land, and all the many outbuildings are almost invisible from the road. The farmhouse itself stands highest, and yet it too is gently hidden, by the surrounding trees. Farming is often the closest form of binding between people and the land. It is no different here, where the Plenderleiths farmed for centuries.

Just along the road to the east, the village of Wiston clambers up the hill, from the old corn mill at the bridge over the Garf Water. Walking uphill through the village would take you past the old mill farmhouse, and cottages, and even up through the dense, mature beechwoods, to farmsteadings and cottages overlooking the valley from above the trees.

It was in Wiston that Thomas Minto lived and worked. He was born in 1760, became a weaver, and, at this time, is the earliest recorded Minto in our family wellspring. He married Jean Gray, of Lanark, on 6th July 1788. They set up home together in Renstruther, (now spelt Ravenstruther), where he continued to ply his trade of weaving. Two very significant events occurred in August of the following year. Jean was safely delivered of a firstborn son, James Minto, and the French Revolution began. Of the two, I suspect that the birth of James probably made much the bigger impact on the household.

James followed his father into the weaving trade, also working from a loom in Ravenstruther, (pronounced Renstry). However, none of James's children knew their grandfather, as James married Elizabeth Anderson a year after his father's death, (from "palsy"), on 13th August 1825. Remarkably for the time, it appears that only one of Elizabeth's eight children died in infancy. The fourth child was called Robert, and was born on 8th April 1833.

Although we have tarried with this family for three generations, now, they haven't moved far during that period. Robert Minto became a railway worker, and later an agricultural labourer based in Ravenstruther. Here, still within sight of Tinto, he married Rutherford Young of Lanark, with whom he had ten children. He died on 1st February 1890, aged 56, as a result of injuries sustained in an accident on the railway at Carstairs Lodge.

We'll hear much more about Thomas Minto of Wiston's later descendants in forthcoming chapters. Meantime, to take us back south towards Tinto again, there is the touch of a real-life tale, well-told, when we consider two of Thomas's great great grand-daughters. These Minto sisters, during the summers of 1908, and 1909 respectively, (about 150 years after Thomas's time), married two Plenderleith brothers, one from Sornfallow farm, and the other from Burnhouse, and so moved back into the Wiston area of their ancestors.

A little to the west of Wiston, is the site of the 17th century Greenhill Farmhouse. It became a significant place during the time of the Covenanters. The 17th Century was a time of great political and religious unrest. This was expressed in England as the civil war between Royalists and Parliamentarians. In Scotland the conflict was between the Royalists and Covenanters. It was really the battle between Presbyterian religious freedom and the issue of "Royal Supremacy in Causes Ecclesiastical" enshrined in Charles I's code of canons.

Charles I sought, by introduction of Episcopy, to put an end to the Presbyterian form of church government. The National Covenant was a document which many thousands of Scots signed, in 1638, in response to this threat.

Professor Ted Cowan, of Glasgow University, describes this as one of the major moments in Scottish history . . . "a supremely important radical departure, because here you had people taking responsibility for their own actions by signing their names on a contract . . . It was a totally new exercise in civic humanism . . . It marked, in a very real sense, the end of the medieval world".

Greenhill Farmhouse was a friendly haven for those preachers who attended field conventicles (open air religious services) in the surrounding moors. Because of this, the house was raided by government troops, on several occasions. Over the forthcoming centuries it crumbled to a roofless shell. But then, beginning in 1975, it was transferred, stone by stone, to Biggar, where it has aptly become that town's Covenanting Museum.

If we continue circling the lower slopes, we come to Scaut Hill in the south east. This hill is a spur projecting from Tinto's main bulk, and is the site of the remains of the strangely named Fatlips Castle. In truth, not much is known about this 16th century rectangular tower house. It may originally have been a Turnbull Hold, and it's a fair guess that it received it's name due to the physical appearance of one of it's early owners.

It was small-holdings such as these that produced the moss-trooper heroes of the middle-ages. Fatlips Castle would have been an important location at that time, as it commanded the Great Western Road.

A local legend relates that, at one time the Laird of Symington owned Fatlips Castle. This Laird subjected his neighbour, the Laird of Lamington, to continual jeering, about the fact that Fatlips Castle overlooked Lamington Tower. Finally, pushed beyond the limit of his tolerance, the Laird of Lamington constructed a brand new home, up the Cowgill. In reality, it is unlikely that this keep was ever occupied by Symington, who was proprietor of the lands of Tintoside. The Tower-house was small, and given the difficulties of access, and the elevation of the site, it is likely that a minor vassal of Symington may have lived here at that time.

Lamington tower, too, is a place touched by the comings and goings of history. A copse of trees hides it's secrets now, and ancient tree stumps guard the gate. Though now a place of nesting corbies, and tumbled stone, seven hundred years ago it was the home of Marion Braidfoot. She was the daughter of the Laird of Lamington, and often stayed at her father's town-house in Lanark. It was probably while visiting here, that she first met her love, and future husband – William Wallace.

It is thought that Wallace rested his men near Lanark in September 1296, after his successful ambush of the English at Loudon Hill where, although outnumbered, he made the land work for him. This led to the defeat of the English, and the death of their leader, Sir John Fenwick, who had executed Wallace's father some years earlier.

Local tradition tells that it was while lying low at Lanark that Wallace met the 18-year old Marion for the first time. They fell in love, and before much more time passed they were married in St. Kentigern's.

The Sheriff of Lanark was a man called Sir William Heselrig, and as commander of the English occupation forces, he had, not long before, hung Marion's brother, Hugh. This, of course, was not an action likely to endear him to William Wallace, who in turn stepped up his covert campaign of guerrilla activity against the enemy.

Sometimes the inevitability of tragedy is what makes it hard to bear. This pressure couldn't keep building forever, without something giving way. It was on a Sunday morning in May 1297 that the violence erupted irrevocably. A running battle on the streets of Lanark left the English troops beaten, with over 50 dead. Wallace and his men escaped, so locals say, to Cartland Crags. But Marion was not so lucky. She was caught, and Heselrig executed her as prompt retribution.

Fueled by grief, Wallace led his force back to Lanark that night, overpowered the garrison, and killed Heselrig. Henceforth, he went on to attack the English wherever he could, determined to defeat the forces of Edward I once and for all.

And while Wallace strides thru' time towards his own tragic end, perhaps he sometimes pauses at Lamington Tower, to listen to the wind sing a gentle lament for Marion among the stones. I know I have so listened.

However far back we tread, as we walk around Tinto, we still find evidence of people at work – and sometimes we have no idea what they were up to. Our journey around the skirts of the hill bring us next to Park Knowe. Happily mystery still exists in many places in the world. This is one of those places. As yet no one is sure what this puzzling monument is. It is situated on the top of a small hill to the east of the main Tinto path. It is oval, and measures about 65 yards by 55 yards, within two banks. The banks are exceptionally thin, and consist of a stone and earth core, kerbed on both sides with a single course of stones. Many of the stones in the kerbs are angular slabs set on edge.

It is possible that the whole structure dates from the time of the Kingdom of the Brythonic people, (the Britons). These were a Celtic people speaking a language akin to Welsh, whose capital was at the Rock of Clyde (Alclwyd), Dumbarton Rock. They endured as a kingdom from the time of the Romans leaving, right up until the battle of Carham in 1018.

Was Park Knowe one of their places. No proof has ever been produced. And the purpose of the structure is just as obscure. Due to the slightness of the banks this monument cannot be classed as a fort. There are no traces of houses, so it isn't considered a settlement.

Therefore Park Knowe remains a mystery, and can be enjoyed by anyone who might wish it to be anything. For everyone from readers of romantic fiction, to sci-fi film aficionados, this site is special, because it isn't harnessed. The flip-side of not knowing what it was, is that it could be many things, limited only by the breadth of your imagination.

Fallburn Fort lies just to the left of the path to Tinto's summit, and is bothered by no crisis of identity. It is most definitely an Iron Age strongpoint. The time is about 650 BC, and the Celtic Warlords have arrived. With them comes the secret of iron production and the use of the blacksmith's forge. This is what assists them in their expansion from homelands in the part of Europe now called Austria. They battle their way into lands stretching from the Black Sea to northern Scotland. And with them comes a new feature in the landscape. The Celtic hillfort begins appearing on defensible, high ground sites.

Fallburn Fort is an excellent example of this type of structure. It is circular, and measures about 70 yards by 60 yards, within double ramparts and ditches. The defences are in a pretty good state of repair, with the inner rampart standing about 10 feet in height and being topped by the remains of a wall about 10 feet thick. The wall probably represents a strengthening of defences during a later phase of occupation.

The Celts were a warlike people, and they usually prepared their defenses well. The particular tribe in the Tinto area at this time were the Damnonii, who later merged with other tribes to become the Britons of Strathclyde.

After Fallburn Fort, the time has probably come to leave the lower slopes, and head up the path, towards the summit of this beacon hill. A famous, but anonymous, rhyme tells us that "on Tintock tap there is a mist, and in that mist there is a kist".

What there certainly is on Tinto's top is one of the largest Bronze age cairns in Scotland. At 20 feet high by 50 yards in diameter, it is enormous. The commanding location which it occupies is the meeting point of the boundaries of no fewer than four parishes.

The Bronze Age settlers arrived in the Clyde Valley by about 2,000 BC. They brought a number of important innovations, such as individual burial of their dead, and a style of pottery known as Beaker Ware. But chief among their secrets was the art of metalworking. They could wrest metal from the earth, and shape it to their own purposes. This included the use of copper and bronze for their tools and weapons, and gold for ornamentation.

The settlers, sometimes called Beaker People, lived in huts of wood and stone. These were often located on hillsides, where drainage was better. There is evidence that they may have worked the copper and gold deposits at Leadhills, south of Tinto.

Leadhills did not, however, have any tin deposits, and nor did anywhere else in Scotland. Tin is an essential ingredient of bronze, and therefore the really big innovation that the bronze-workers brought was the necessity for international trade.

Before the Bronze Age, the plains below this summit were the home to various Stone Age peoples. The farmers of the New Stone Age have left some significant structures in the flatter lands to the north east.

Earlier yet, in the days of the primal forests, the nomadic hunters of the Old Stone Age left little sign of their passing. The only evidence that they were here, at all, is in their stone axes, flint tools, and arrowheads, found in numbers near the River Clyde.

Nowadays, of course, these wide lands around the skirts of Tinto, are laced with modern roads, and houses. We see trains passing through, and off to the west we can see the broad ribbon of the southbound motorway. On the fields of farms like Sornfallow, we see tractors, and even Quad bikes moving busily. And above, the skies are the province of those leisure-seekers, on modern wings.

One day, many years before micro-lights and hang-gliders were even invented, Tinto was resting quietly in the afternoon sunshine. Nothing was moving on the path around the top edge of Maurice's Cleugh. This steep-sided corrie on the north side of the hill runs down into the fields and woods of Carmichael Parish. The world was motionless, and even the undergrowth was still. The first hint that something was coming was a disturbance in the air. This was followed by the sound of feet pounding along the path. Minutes later we burst into view, my father and me, laughing like idiots, and doing "for stupid" what those microlights and hang-gliders would do "for real", decades later. We were flying on Tinto.

"Flying on Tinto" involved pounding along the track above the Corrie of Maurice's Cleugh, and when the ground opened up beneath our feet, throwing our arms wide, and raising our heads and eyes to the heavens. It was then that you could feel the thermals catch you and lift you upwards, leaving the ground hundreds of feet below. You could see the fields and woods passing beneath you. Then reality would hit, and the operation was completed by falling backwards a couple of feet, onto the heathery bank, laughing, in complete safety, still yards from any drop-off.

The earlier discussions that we had had at Lanark Loch that morning were now put temporarily aside. The early morning mists had cleared, and fun was the order of the day. And yet, all unknown at that time, it was still a lesson. A lesson in the power of imagination, and in the way in which we can mould the world into unexpected shapes.

Most of all it was a lesson in the strength of self, and also the need for a sense of the ridiculous.

What I was given that day was the secret of the power of flight. Memory is a chancy thing, and the world through a twelve year old's eyes is not the same as that which surrounds a forty-four year old. But as near as I can remember, the secret is this: *that things really can be as you wish to see them, and if you are prepared to let a little magic into the mix, you won't be disappointed in the result. Take the step, because only you can make it happen.*

That secret may sound a little far-fetched and new-age, but I don't believe it to be so. As Clydesdale times move forward through the eighteenth century we get closer to the point where people upped and left for the new world(s).

The line of least resistance for most people is to stay put. As we have seen, people "stayed put" in the Clyde Valley from Neolithic times. They were joined, and strengthened by successive waves of settlers from elsewhere. But once here, it seems that the surroundings were attractive and productive enough to keep the population from straying further. It is often the case, in general, that such a condition of contentment is usually only changed either by the use of external force – (physical and/or economic), or by internal force – (the secret of flying) – using both strength and curiosity to take the big step.

The big step was coming, and different people would take it for different reasons, but I like to think that Tinto, (or it's equivalent), was there, somewhere, behind every decision, giving confidence in that step, away from solid ground.

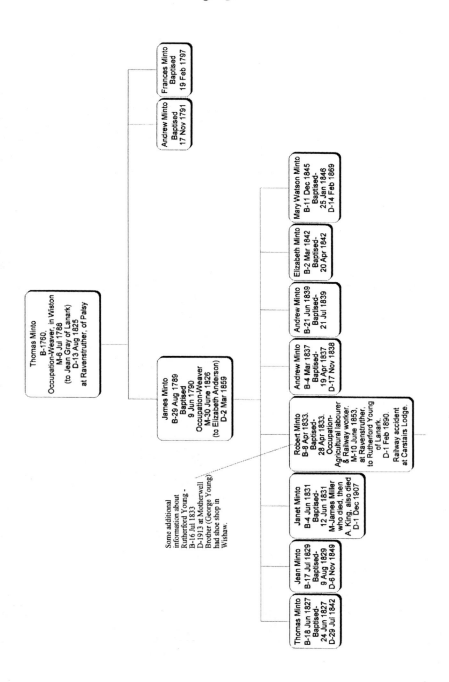

Thomas Minto
B-1760,
Occupation-Weaver, in Wiston
M-6 Jul 1788
(to Jean Gray of Lanark)
D-13 Aug 1825
at Ravenstruther, of Paisy

Andrew Minto
Baptised
17 Nov 1791

Frances Minto
Baptised
19 Feb 1797

James Minto
B-29 Aug 1789
Baptised
9 Jun 1790
Occupation-Weaver
M-30 June 1826
(to Elizabeth Anderson)
D-2 Mar 1859

Some additional
information about
Rutherford Young -
B-16 Jul 1833
D-1913 at Motherwell
Brother (George Young)
had shoe shop in
Wishaw.

Thomas Minto
B-18 Jun 1827
Baptised-
24 Jun 1827
D-29 Jul 1842

Jean Minto
B-17 Jul 1829
Baptised-
9 Aug 1829
D-6 Nov 1849

Janet Minto
B-4 Jun 1831
Baptised-
12 Jun 1831
M-James Miller
who died, then
A. King, also died
D-1 Dec 1907

Robert Minto
B-8 Apr 1833.
Baptised-
28 Apr 1833.
Occupation-
Agricultural labourer
& Railway worker.
M-10 June 1853,
at Ravenstruther,
to Rutherford Young
of Lanark.
D-1 Feb 1890.
Railway accident
at Carstairs Lodge.

Andrew Minto
B-4 Mar 1837.
Baptised-
19 Apr 1837
D-17 Nov 1838

Andrew Minto
B-21 Jun 1839
Baptised-
21 Jul 1839

Elizabeth Minto
B-2 Mar 1842
Baptised-
20 Apr 1842

Mary Watson Minto
B-11 Dec 1845
Baptised-
25 Jan 1846
D-14 Feb 1869

Mintos – from Thomas (born 1760) to Robert (Died 1890).

Chapter Two

Paisley Patterns

"Oh, what a tangled web we weave"
Sir Walter Scott

As I rise slowly from sleep, morning light seeps between the curtains, and fills the room, giving it the look of backlit monochrome film. Peering from newly wakened eyes, everything looks a little grey and washed out. It takes a moment for the mind to make sense of shapes dimly seen by half-light, and the detail that always seems to come last to the picture is colour. Strangely though, my tie, hanging over the back of my chair, is one of the few items in the room to prove the exception to that rule. Its colour shows through, even at those black and white times of the day. That might be due to the material, or the weave. Or it might be due to the colour which is a luminous light blue, with a strong and distinctive pattern of Purple teardrop shapes – a Paisley Pattern.

Paisley, often described as the largest town in Scotland, occupies an important position in our story. The threads from this town's past run outwards across the oceans, where, in faraway lands, the warp and the weft from this Renfrewshire place have changed the world. The warp are the loom's longwise threads, and the weft are the crosswise threads, and while they remain in order, and in place, the end pattern can be predicted. But when they tangle, as in life, the future becomes a mystery.

The development of the textile mills in Paisley really are recent history. Like Upper Clydesdale, this area has been settled for millennia. To begin at the beginning would take us back to the Stone Age, and perhaps that's a little far. So instead, let's look, (very quietly), at the hunter just below the summit ridge of the Gleniffer Braes, at the "beginning of the end" of the Age of the Forest.

He is a Celt, of the Damnonii tribe, and related to those living at Fallburn on Tinto. Unlike Tinto, which borders on the lands of the Selgovae, this isn't frontier country. So rather than being battle-ready, he's out hunting, for Wild Boar. Some of the animals are moving, through the trees, below him and don't suspect the presence of the hunters, closing in on them. While he waits for his fellows to get into position, he ensures that he is noiselessly settled, downwind of the prey, and below the skyline. Then, reassured that all is well, he looks around.

The woods are still thick, here in the basin of the Clyde, (or Clwyd, as he says, in his Welsh-related Celtic tongue). Oak, Ash and Elm grow thickly on the lowlands, and birch and rowan thrive here, on the braes. But these woods are under constant and sustained attack, by his people. He can see the ropes of smoke rising from a score of places across the forest, where many communities are using the fine new iron axes to clear swathes of trees. Farms are created in the opened areas, and the felled trees are used to feed the forge, and build the house. And in some places, the constructions are even more impressive, with whole palisades and fortifications created from timber. If he stretches up, a little more, and squints north, he thinks he might just see the vast rock that marks his people's capital – Alclwyd. Stretching so, his foot slips, twigs crack! and "dinner" takes to its hairy heels, amidst the still-thick woods.

Within a few generations the blanketing forest is gone. To the north, the Great Wood of Caledon still covers large stretches of the valleys and flatlands. But here, by the Clyde, it has been broken into smaller stretches of woods, separated by open land. By now it has been harvested not only by the Damnonii, but also by the invading Romans.

In 80 AD, Agricola had crossed the Solway-Tyne line. His two massive armoured columns churned northwards from both Corbridge and Carlisle. The measured tread of thousands of troops made the ground shake, and made the people think carefully. The Damnonii, together with some other tribes, cautiously cooperated with the Romans. By 82 AD the central lands were quiet. The Carynx, (the Celtic battle horn), was silenced, and the people lived under Pax Romana.(the Peace of Rome).

These southern and central tribes watched with a wary interest then, when Agricola marched north across the Highland Line. There, their cousins, the warlike Caledonii, held sway. Rome, as the common enemy, had had the effect of forging the northern tribes into a united force. It is said that as Agricola marched north, he was opposed by an army of Caledonians thirty thousand strong. They were led by the earliest named of the Scottish heroes, – Calgacus, (or in the Celtic tongue – "Calgath"), meaning swordsman. Calgacus' speech, when speaking to the tribes, has echoed down the centuries:

" . . . To us who dwell on the uttermost confines of the earth and of freedom, this remote sanctuary of Britain's glory has up to this time been a defence. But now, the farthest bounds of Britain lie open to our enemies. There are no other people beyond us, nothing indeed but waves and rocks, and the yet more terrible Roman Fleet. Robbers of the world, having by their universal plunder exhausted the land they rifle the deep . . . To robbery, slaughter, plunder, they give the lying name of Empire; they make a desolation and call it peace."

Whether the words are really attributable to him, (or are a literary addition by Tacitus, son-in-law of Agricola and recorder of the northern campaigns), the fact remains that these words have long been inspirational. They have helped to shape the stubborn bloody-mindedness and independent spirit of the Scottish psyche. There is a strong echo over a thousand years later, in 1320, in the words of the Declaration of Arbroath:

" . . . For as long as one hundred of us shall remain alive we shall never in any wise consent to submit . . . "

Although the Romans never conquered the Highlands, they intermittently occupied southern and central Scotland throughout the following few years. In 143 AD the Damnonii again heard axes at work, in great numbers, in their woods. The Emperor, Antonius Pius, was building a wall, right through their territories. A wall constructed mainly of wood. A wall six metres high, and thirty-seven miles long, defended by heavy wooden battlements, and nineteen forts. The axes were busy for a long time, and the forests took the toll. And yet, only twenty years later, this "Antonine Wall" lay broken and abandoned.

Thereafter the Romans remained mostly in the safe provinces, south of Hadrian's wall, and when the last of the Legions quit Britain around 410 AD, the northern tribes hardly noticed. The Damnonii were grateful for new metalworking and crafts skills, but otherwise the Roman influence was light.

Perhaps it was these new skills that led to the Damnonii, within decades of the Roman departure, becoming the driving force in the emerging kingdom of the Britons of Strathclyde. This Kingdom stretched from Carlisle to Loch Lomond, and centred on the great basalt rock, at Dumbarton.

There are records of St Patrick writing to Ceretic, the earliest known ruler of Strathclyde, around 450 AD. Later, in 560 AD, an Irish Monk, called Mirin, founded a Celtic church at Seedhill, within what later became known as Paisley. Tales of miracles soon made St. Mirin's shrine a popular place of pilgrimage.

The next few centuries were turbulent, in the extreme. The land we know now as Scotland was home to four different peoples, and they were all intent on carving ever bigger territories. Internecine warfare raged, in all combinations, between the Scots, the Picts, the Angles, and the Britons.

Then, in 795 AD, came that freeze-frame moment. The four battlers paused, in disbelief. You could have heard a political pin drop! A fifth team had entered the game, all uninvited, and worse still, they were ruthless and effective, these Vikings.

The Norse and Danish invaders harried the coastlines of the country unmercifully. In the face of this threat, the Celtic peoples of the land drew ever closer to each other, the Scots and Picts finally uniting under Kenneth MacAlpin in 843 AD.

Artgal, king of the Britons was faced with catastrophe in 871 AD. The Vikings, Ivar the Boneless, and Olaf the White, combined forces, and fell upon Strathclyde, with two hundred galleys. They plundered the countryside and sacked Dumbarton, taking many Britons with them, into slavery, when they returned to their base in Dublin.

Dumbarton Rock today – The Rock of Clyde, (Alclwyd).

Artgal's son, Rhun, ruled Strathclyde for a further five years, but it was a kingdom on its knees. It never really recovered from the "Great Raid" of 871 AD, and became part of the rest of Scotland on Rhun's death in 877 AD. Rhun's son succeeded to the Scottish throne, due to Rhun's earlier marriage to the daughter of Kenneth MacAlpin.

As the importance of Dumbarton declined, other places within the lands around the Clyde estuary rose to prominence. In 1163 a community of thirteen Cluniac monks, a variant on the Benedictine order, set up a monastery near St. Mirin's shrine. This was by invitation from Walter Fitzalan, the first hereditary High Steward of Scotland, and, in 1219, the monastery became Paisley Abbey.

The Norsemen continued to raid the west coast of Scotland throughout this time. All of the Western Isles and much of Argyll had become their sovereign territory. They continued to trouble Scotland until the middle of the thirteenth century.

The last great Viking offensive was the attack by King Haakon of Norway in 1263. He sailed for Scotland with a vast fleet, (the greatest force that had ever left Norway). It was a campaign beset by troubles. The fleet mustered off Kerrera too late in the year, and by the time they entered the Firth of Clyde it was already Autumn. Then, during negotiation with Alexander III, an October storm hit, causing havoc with the fleet. Finally, when Haakon sent men ashore to refloat some of his beached vessels, they were attacked by the Scots army. This was the famous Battle of Largs, and the result was inconclusive. It was, however, the last armed clash between Norway and the Scottish Crown. Peace followed, with the signing of the Treaty of Perth in 1266.

There continue, of course, to be many people of Norse ancestry living up and down the western seaboard, to this day. With many west-coasters it's a case of – scratch the surface, find the Viking beneath.

One old tradition states that the name Allison is derived from early Scandinavian settlers on the Clyde coast, and that it is an Anglicisation of the name Olafsson. This is also the oft attributed root for the Allisons of northern, and north-eastern, Scotland.

Many other families claim Viking descent, but they have written records which clarify their origins. Even Clan Donald have significant Norse heritage, descending from Somerled's wife, the Princess Ragnhilda. She was the daughter of Olaf the Red, King of the Isle of Man, who was, in turn, descended from the Kings of Norway.

The earliest offshoot of Clan Donald is the Clan MacAlister. They descend from Alastair Mor, younger son of Donald I of the Isles, (for whom the MacDonalds are named). They are worthy of mention within our tale, as they represent another possible source of the surname – Allison.

Alistair Mor's descendants became known as the MacAlisters of Loup, (an area of Kintyre south of West Loch Tarbert). The chief, in Kintyre, misguidedly supported Edward I of England during the Scottish Wars of Independence in the 14th century.

It is said that some of these MacAlisters escaped from their Clanlands, fled to Avondale in Lanarkshire, and later changed their name to Allison. Our ancestral Allisons seem to hail from Renfrewshire, however. That is certainly where they are living when we first make their acquaintance. Thus, a third possibility is that our brand of Allison descends from MacAllan. This would certainly make a linguistic sense, as the initial english translation would be Allanson, which is but a short step from Alason.

We have already heard of the Lanark exploits of the hero, William Wallace. He is also strongly associated with Renfrewshire. He is said to have been born in the village of Elderslie, and very possibly educated in the nearby Abbey of Paisley. The lands were, at that time still in the hands of the Fitzalan family, who had changed their name to Stewart, to reflect their hereditary office. The fifth High Steward, Walter Stewart, married Marjory Bruce, daughter of Robert the Bruce, in 1315. She died the next year, in Paisley Abbey Infirmary, following a riding accident nearby. She was pregnant at the time, but the child was saved, and later became Robert II, first of the Stewart Kings. The Abbey is burial place to six High Stewards, Marjory Bruce, Robert II's wives, and Robert III.

Paisley did well in the time of the Stewarts. It even became a Burgh of Barony in 1488, thanks to James IV. Following this, the burgesses had the right to hold regular markets and fairs, and the burgh continued to develop, in medieval street pattern, from the Abbey outwards. In fact, as recently as 1990 a stretch of 90 metres of original medieval drain was found near there.

Up until the mid-sixteenth century the bonds between Burgh and Abbey were tightly tied, and any professional developments were strictly planned and controlled. The Reformation changed all that, cutting cords between Church and Commerce, and preparing the town for the birth of many new guilds and trades. These included weaving, and dyeing, amongst many others. Paslay, (as it was then known), was beginning the journey upon the road to recognition as one of the world's leading textile centres.

By the late seventeenth century the town was a thriving hub of activity and trade, and had overtaken Renfrew as the main centre of the surrounding fertile agricultural area. Part of its rich hinterland was the parish of Houston and Killellan. This area lies almost midway between the Gleniffer Braes and the Rock of Dumbarton. It is fertile, and yet well-wooded, and steeply undulating. The oldest surviving church building is the ruined Kirk of Kilallan, which bears the date of 1635. This ruin is situated in Barochan Cross Road about four miles northwest of the centre of Houston.

Was it close to here, later that same century that James Alason was born? It seems likely. The records show him living in Erskine, and becoming married to Janet Patoun of Killellan on 16th November 1711. Aspects of her life probably took place in the Kirk of Kilallan.

The first of James and Janet's four children, Walter, was born on 31st August 1712. At some point in his lifetime the spelling of his surname was recorded differently from his father, and so he is found to be Walter Allason. Although there is little firm written evidence, clues and hints lead to the conclusion that the Allasons were, at this time involved in agriculture.

It is during this same period in the eighteenth century that the nearby town became known by its modern name of Paisley. Its textile industry was developing apace, with the construction of areas like Shuttle Street, which was built about 1735, to provide houses for the handloom weavers, who traditionally always worked from their own homes.

Walter married Agnes Erskine in 1743, and they had five children. Agnes was carrying their second child when news came of the approach of the Jacobite Army, in 1745. The area was in uproar. The town of Paisley was especially worried, having been a loyal supporter of the Hanoverian Government. On Saturday 28th December it became known that the Jacobites were only seven miles away in Glasgow.

Local farmers and agricultural workers, such as the Allasons, drove all the local cattle to hide in the hills around Lochwinnoch, to save them from the hungry Jacobite army.

The Army did arrive, albeit the next day, and Bonnie Prince Charlie required that Paisley pay a fine of £1000, to ensure it's immunity to looting and pillage. With much difficulty, and in part due to the assistance of a local benefactor, this community of only four thousand people did manage to make the adjusted payment of £500. The Jacobites passed on to the south, marching with almost unseemly haste, towards the doom that awaited their cause.

The third Allason child was born in 1751, and was also called Walter, after his father. As this Walter grew, his surname underwent yet another shift, and emerged in the form that we know it today – he became known as Walter Allison.

Walter was a Farmer in Houston and Killellan Parish, and was courting Janet Ersdon in 1776. Meantime, on the other side of the Atlantic, big things had been happening. The year before, 1775, saw the fire of the American Revolution being stoked, and it flared in 1776, when they gave their Declaration of Independence to the world.

Would these events have intruded on Walter and Janet? The answer is "Almost certainly." Almost half of the signers of the document were of Scots descent. One of its architects, the Reverend John D. D. Witherspoon, had been a well-loved preacher in Paisley until his emigration in 1768.

This same man later became the first President of Princeton College, New Jersey. Here he trained the leadership of that new country in all of the common-sense philosophies of the Scottish enlightenment, such as the concept of the people reigning supreme. Here is one of the best examples of that Paisley warp and weft, running through the larger weave.

Stubborn bloody-mindedness and independence of spirit make another appearance here too, as we again consider the words attributed to Calgacus, and how their echoes have not only shaped the development of Scotland, but also America.

1. Calgacus :

"This field is to decide whether to endure the penalties of an enslaved people for ever, or instantly avenge them. Think therefore, as you advance to battle, at once of your ancestors and of your posterity".

2. Declaration of Arbroath :

"Yet if he should give up what he has begun, and should seek to make us or our kingdom subject to . . . the English, we would strive at once to drive him out as our enemy and a subverter of his own right and ours", . . .

3. Declaration of Independence :

"All Men are endowed by their Creator with certain inalienable Rights, That among these are Life, Liberty and the Pursuit of Happiness – whenever any Form of Government becomes destructive of these Ends, it is the Right of the People to alter or to abolish it", . . .

Thus, the same principles appear and reappear. The importance of Liberty, the rights of the People, and the concept of Elective Leadership – (removeable if necessary). All three documents, therefore, enshrine what may be viewed as the earliest known form of rugged constitutionalism.

The American revolutionary war pulled in Scots on both sides. One of the early engagements was the Battle of Moore's Creek, and it perfectly exemplifies the ambiguous place of Scots in the struggle. There were highlanders among the American patriots, but possibly even more among the British loyalists. This battle is, in fact, often called America's Culloden, due to the numbers of kilted Scots involved, fighting with broadswords and bagpipes. Scots who fought with the loyalists were later encouraged to emigrate again, this time to Canada.

The ordinary people in Scotland would have been aware of events in America. People in Renfrewshire, too, would have an interest in the activities of the Reverend Witherspoon. There is therefore a reasonable likelihood that Walter and Janet knew of the Revolutionary activities across the sea. These faraway happenings wouldn't, however, have interfered with the ebb and flow of their usual life. They were married the following year, in 1777, and proceeded to have at least ten children that are recorded. The eighth of these was Samuel Allison, born on 19th March, 1792.

This was the fourth generation of Alasons/Allisons born in the Erskine area. Scotland was in the midst of both the Age of Enlightenment, and the Industrial Revolution, (both of which we'll hear more of, later). In France 1792 was the year of the abolition of the Monarchy, but baby Samuel didn't care. His top priority was getting a fair share of anything going, despite having seven elder siblings.

I am moved to wonder anew about that early Celtic hunter. If he had been blessed with second sight, how much of this tangled web would he have sensed, as he stretched to see, before the twig snapped, and brought him tumbling back to reality.

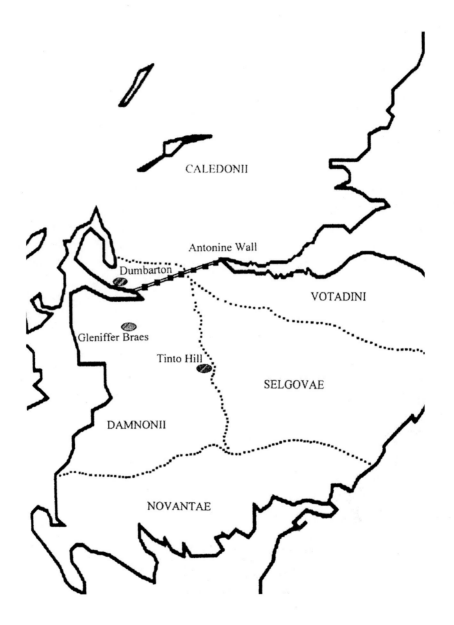

CALEDONII

Antonine Wall

Dumbarton

VOTADINI

Gleniffer Braes

Tinto Hill

SELGOVAE

DAMNONII

NOVANTAE

The Central Belt of Scotland, and Early Peoples.

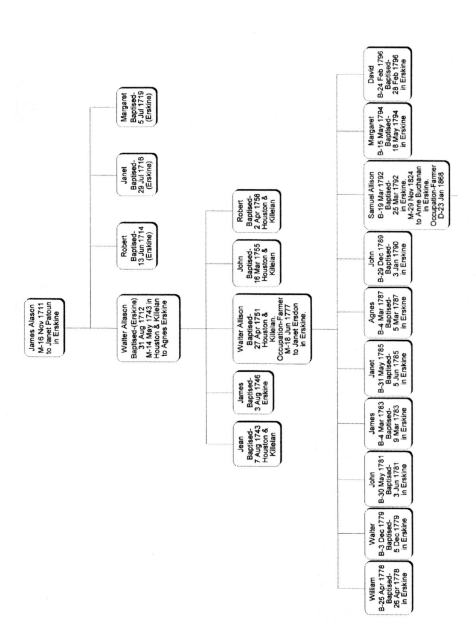

Allisons – from James (married 1711) to Samuel (Died 1868).

Chapter Three

Staying Put

*"The land was forever, it moved and
changed below you, but was forever"*
Lewis Grassic Gibbon

The snow is falling heavily on Drummossie Moor, this February 1747. The moor is the site of the battle of Culloden, and the snow barely hides those scars and mounds in the earth that mark the pits where the fallen were piled in their hundreds. Scarcely a year has passed since that decimation of a generation of Scots, and already the land has changed. Fear and fire reign. Executions, forfeitures, proscriptions, and fines have all served to lay a heavy yoke of oppression across the country.

The '45 was a civil war, and now, in its aftermath, there are few winners in Scotland. Those that fought for King George II have been subject to the same draconian measures as those that fought for the Stuarts. I doubt if Justice has ever been blinder. Westminster seems to be too far away to tell the difference between Highlander and Lowlander, or Jacobite and Hanoverian.

As the situation worsens, the inevitable occurs. Fast-forward two years, and pull right back, to bring the whole country into view. An emigrant ship is leaving. The first of many such. The Highlanders are at the forefront of this exodus, but they are by no means alone. Tens of thousands of Scots continue to leave their straths and glens through the rest of the eighteenth and nineteenth centuries.

Some are fugitives, and some are visionaries seeking a fuller life elsewhere, whilst still others are the displaced and the dispossessed. Many are ordinary men, leaving their homes, and following the soldier's life, in order to feed their wives and children.

Many of these men of the Highland Regiments have another reason too, for serving in faraway lands. They are a people whose whole world has been so expunged that enlisting in the perilous trade of military service is the only means by which the "Mother of Parliaments" in Westminster will permit them to speak their language, or play their music.

See the ships leaving from ports all round the country. Hear the lament rising, and filling the air. It comes from those aboard, and it is matched by those onshore, who wait and watch, until the promise for the future, (the next generation), is hull-down on the horizon, never to return. Colonist's ships, prison ships, and troopships all have one thing in common. They leave full and return empty.

Even looking only at troopships the numbers are almost beyond belief. Before the eighteenth century draws to a close, thirty four battalions have marched from the glens. Most of them will not march back. The haemorrhage is widespread. As the nineteenth century progresses, and the Highland Clearances begin in earnest, tens of thousands are lost. The wonder is that there is enough lifeblood left, to keep the country functioning at all. And yet function it does. There are many, both bright and capable, who can, and do, choose to stay. There is one kind of strength needed in those who go, and another kind of strength needed by those who stay, and we will look at the fervour and determination required by both, in later chapters within this tale.

We shall soon hear of some of the family Minto, and the family Allison, who choose to walk farther afield in the world seeking a new life for their dependants. Many others from the same wellspring choose to stay put however, striving to create a better future here at home, for their families, and for their land.

The latter half of the eighteenth century, and the bulk of the nineteenth, are darkened by the national disgrace of the Clearances, especially throughout the north. They are also, however, characterised elsewhere by significant improvements and developments in social structure, agriculture, industry, transportation and economy.

Beginning somewhere between 1730 and 1750, the Age of Enlightenment heralded a new renaissance across Scotland, with Edinburgh becoming known as The Athens of the north. This era lasted until the end of the century. If the "Romantic Age" is included, then the time-frame could be seen as having extended into the 1830's. This period was characterised by a creative explosion in the arts and sciences, literature and philosophy, unparalleled anywhere before or since. It changed, forever, the way we view ourselves, and the world around us. The "roll call of honour" of the times contains long lists of names of people now viewed as exceptional in their fields. These include Adam Smith, Thomas Carlyle, Robert Burns, Sir Walter Scott, David Hume, Hugh Miller, and Joseph Black.

The Age of Enlightenment was sometimes called the great leap forward, especially in the sciences. These advances led to a number of new ways of doing things. This was probably due to the fact that these "literati" didn't just talk the talk, they also walked the walk. They were prepared to innovate, implementing developments that led directly to the "agricultural improvers" and the Industrial Revolution".

The many improvements in agriculture were caused partly by the intellectual curiosity of the age, and partly by the necessity of a country in conflict. Britain was almost permanently at war throughout the eighteenth century, and indeed up until 1815. The result was a military machine hungry for grain, and for cattle. Scotland was under pressure to deliver this, and this sped the process of improvement. "The Honourable Society of Improvers in the Knowledge of Agriculture" was founded in 1723. The following century saw the formation of a flight of intelligent and informed steps, which included the use of lime and fertiliser, crop rotation, stock enclosure, animal husbandry, and mechanisation.

Mechanisation also changed forever the way that people worked, ushering in the Industrial Revolution.

Industry, in one form or another, had been known in Scotland for millennia. In a flash of ancestor overlay, we can be simultaneously behind the eyes of the Bronze Age cairnbuilder, on Tinto, and the Iron Age Hunter, on the Gleniffer Braes. Both are looking out over the forests of the Clyde Basin, and both can see the tell tale blue-grey ribbons of smoke threading upwards from various places amidst the trees. Some of these rise from cookfires, but some mark the places where men labour carefully, smelting marvels from the base metals of the earth.

In a later era, James VI was treated to a tour of the sixteenth century undersea Coal Mines at Culross. It was an unusual visit, which fed his already active paranoia.

James was, of course, the ninth monarch in a dynasty beset by manipulation, betrayal and murder. We can therefore forgive his panic attack, when he was taken up the Culross mine shaft, to be shown how it opened on an artificial island far from shore. His cries of "murder!, treachery!" echoed across the Forth. It took George Bruce, the mine owner, some considerable time to explain the misunderstanding, and calm the situation down. He was probably lucky to keep his head, in the literal sense.

These tales show industry as being part and parcel of Scottish life through the ages. So, what sets the Industrial Revolution – (1760 to 1820) – aside as different, and noteworthy? More than any single other factor, it is probably an issue of the scale of activity.

The massive increases in industrial enterprise, output, and the numbers of people involved, are due mainly to mechanisation, and a host of scientific improvements in industrial processes brought about as part of the great leap forward. The textiles industry grows significantly, in many towns across Scotland, and linen becomes the country's main export.

In Paisley, the famous "pattern" makes its first appearance in the mid 18th century, fully two hundred and forty years before illuminating my mornings. It had originally been used on shawls in Kashmir, and it is the East India Company who introduce these shawls to Britain. They become hugely popular, but both costly and hard to get. Hence the rush by British textile manufacturers to bring out a cheap imitation. Paisley, in particular, emerges as the principal producer of these shawls. These garments remain very much in demand for seventy years, and the term "Paisley" becomes known worldwide.

Things really kick into high gear with James Watt's invention of an efficient steam engine. This revolutionises mining and mine pumps, and is also used in the operation of presses and mills. In just a few decades it will also power locomotives and steamboats. For now though, it is being used in the establishment of huge new textile mills at a variety of locations including New Lanark on the Clyde, and Spinningdale in Sutherland. These mills are associated with Robert Owen and David Dale, and also with ground-breaking social improvements in the lives of the men, women, and especially children, who work in them.

But these big mills have a downside, other than the long hours that the children are required to work. This large scale mechanisation is not labour intensive, and increasingly, unemployment becomes a social problem.

The old handloom weavers, of whom there are tens of thousands, are badly affected. Mechanised mills mean cheaper goods in competition, and leads to a fall in sales and standard of living for the older craftspeople, like Thomas Minto, and his son James, (page 63 and 000). More and more of the handloom weavers give up, and are absorbed into the ever-growing workforces of the mills.

This may be one of the reasons that Robert Minto, in the next generation, opts for farm and railway work instead. This decision is also probably partly brought on by his dissatisfaction, (as a youth), at being regularly sent to Glasgow, (30 miles distant), on foot, with a bolt of cloth for sale. Paisley was the only main centre where the weaving handcraft continued to flourish, as, at first, the "Paisley Pattern" proved to be too complex for the early power looms.

Before Robert's time though, and just after both James Minto and Samuel Allison had been born, the French Revolution, (which had initially found some favour in Scotland), slid deeper into violence, and ultimately war. These "Napoleonic" Wars were fiercely opposed in Scotland, and were viewed as French Imperialist wars of aggression.

War lasted until 1815, and had a number of consequences – some obvious, others less so. Many Scots served in British regiments throughout Europe, in the years between 1794 and 1815, and many of them fell.

As we have already heard, industry and agriculture could not help but be affected by the country being on war-footing. The farms of

Houston and Killelan Parish helped to feed the troops across the battlefields of Europe. Walter Allison and family found the extra income useful, but at the same time, this didn't diminish the grief they felt for those friends and relatives whom they knew, serving and suffering in the foreign campaigns.

Napoleon, by the famous Berlin decree of 1806, made a direct assault upon the Scottish textile industry. The decree effectively stopped the supply of silk from Europe. The silk thread had been used to make heddles, (a yarn-filled wire loop), for the looms, and without these, the industry could collapse. Two local men, the Clark brothers, experimented with a cotton substitute, the new product was launched in 1812, and a new factory opened. James Clark is credited with the invention of the wooden spool or bobbin.

After Napoleon's final defeat at Waterloo in 1815, the Scottish economy entered a post-war slump, aggravated by large numbers of returning soldiery, with no offers or hopes of employment. These war veterans and their families faced poverty and starvation, and this had a knock-on effect on the country's industrial health. The handloom weavers, previously Scotland's industrial backbone, were under threat from the mills, and everyone in that restless, worrying time could feel the land moving and changing below them.

The weavers were well-educated, and used the time that their "quiet occupation" offered, to debate and discuss. As a result they were particularly open to radical ideas. From 1817 onwards secret societies thrived in back courts, and revolution was the whispered word on the side streets. In 1819 and 1820, the situation intensified, and,inflamed by government "agent provocateurs", what became known as "The Radical War" spilled out, onto many main streets.

There were riots in Glasgow, Greenock, and Paisley, as well as a short-lived uprising at Bonnymuir on 5th April 1820. Of forty seven prisoners taken by the Stirlingshire Yeomanry, three were executed for treason, nineteen were transported to Australia, and the rest were eventually released. The legacy of those who were transported overseas lives on, and we will hear more about them in chapter nine.

Samuel, working as a farm labourer, at this point, would have been largely bypassed by such industrial unrest. He married Anne Buchanan on 29 November 1824, and between 1825 and 1846 they had 10 children. Three of these will continue to be central to our tale of rivers running far. These are : Walter, the eldest of the ten, born in 1825; then John, the fourth child, born in 1831; and finally David, (my own great grandfather),youngest of them all, and born in 1846.

The nineteenth century was a time of contrast, and of contradictions. This was the century when Queen Victoria nurtured and then harvested the interest in the north of Scotland, first sown the century before, by the tours of Thomas Pennant and Samuel Johnson. Paisley, during this period, had built a reputation for literary ability and independent thinking. There is a story which describes a public dinner in the nineteenth century at which a toast was proposed to the "Paisley Poets", and every man present rose up to answer it!

At the same time, it was the century most associated with growth in textiles manufacture, shipbuilding, and heavy industry. While the Highlands were, in the main, untouched by the Industrial Revolution, and became a fashionable tourism destination, the Lowlands, by contrast, became the industrial engine of the country.

The country's population became concentrated in this Central "Belt" and before long, one third of the Scottish manufacturing workforce lived in Lanarkshire. Glasgow, which in 1740, had a population of about 17,000, had become a large city, of 200,000 people, by 1831 – and it would double in size again, over the next 30 years.

By 1828 iron and coal industries were in full swing due to discovery of plentiful blackband ironstone, and the invention of hot blast smelting, This, added to the history of steamship development, was the origin of the Scottish shipbuilding industry.

Henry Bell's Comet, although not the first steamship ever built, was certainly the first commercial open-water steamship in Europe. By 1832, the Clyde shipyards had constructed over 70 steamships. Shipbuilding and marine engineering became, from those beginnings, probably Scotland's single biggest contribution to the Industrial Revolution.

The Comet on the Clyde, (1812).

The century progressed, and with every year, the land changed. At first, very little of this was a force for good. The change was orchestrated by the heavy rhythmic thumping of pistons and drive-shafts, punctuated by the hiss of escaping steam. This symphony was played out, in large and dark factories, where people spent most of their waking lives, in bondage to dangerous machines. Illumination was often provided by the glow of molten rivers, or by the unfettered arc of sparks. The only complaint heard was the shriek of machine-metal on metal, sometimes bursting the eardrums of their young operators.

The thump of the piston drives home image after image, as the rods lift and slam down, creating their own litany, a song of the wrong, and a rhyme of the time. With every impact we see another picture : children pulling carts, like horses, in the dark of the mines; pregnant women leaving their machines only long enough to give birth; endemic rickets and tuberculosis; smallpox; over a million people housed in single-room homes; lack of plumbing or water; cholera epidemics; unemployment; drunkenness; and crime.

This background of poverty and unemployment gave rise to the Chartist movement, which sought a six-point People's Charter – adult male suffrage, secret ballots, equal electoral districts, salaried MPs, abolition of property qualifications, and annual parliaments. A Poor Law Amendment Act for Scotland was passed in 1845, setting a legal poor rate and strengthening workhouse provision.

Little more than two decades had passed since the Radical War, and the towns of the handloom weavers were still hothouses, nourishing and propagating radical ideals, and thus becoming the nurseries of the Chartist cause.

Paisley's Provost, in the 1840's, was a former radical, and was thus prepared to work with the Chartists locally. This was a blessing, when economic disaster struck the town in 1842 and 1843. Over half of the town's businesses went bankrupt, leaving around 15,000 people dependant on charity for even their barest existence. There was little panic or riot, however, as the radical leaders locally, (Robert Cochran and Patrick Brewster), were committed to a moral-force Chartism that rejected violence, and they were prepared to work with the Provost and local relief committee, for the common good.

These same Chartists, and their descendants were graced by that stubborn bloody-mindedness and independence of spirit that I referred to towards the end of Chapter Two. These individualists often felt moved to emigrate, taking with them the concepts of civil liberty, the rights of the people, and the idea of elective leadership. Thus, the young societies in America and Australia were strongly imprinted at an early stage, by Scots egalitarianism, and self-reliance.

The Chartist's petition lost some credibility nationally, after 1847, when a number of its signatures were found to be forged. However, Reform Acts later in the century did incorporate all of the recommendations excepting annual elections.

Until reforms, and that rare beast – the enlightened industrialist, began making a difference, the common man's solution to his sorrows was often to drown them in the demon drink. Legally brewed alcohol was just the countertop part of the problem, and was added to by large amounts of poteen, (moonshine), distilled everywhere from urban tenement to country glen. In 1840, surveys indicated that the Scots were, on annual average, downing six times as much volume in spirits, as the English.

Walter Allison was, sadly, one of those who had long since left even the world of average behind. He was, by the 1850's, living in Cathcart, and had some difficulties handling the change in the land below him. His response was to become a chronic alcoholic. And worse, he was no "happy drinker". His son, John, described him as "causing considerable anguish when drunk". Thus, Walter's children often stayed with their grandparents, sometimes grandmother Smith, and sometimes Ann and Samuel, in Erskine. Some of the children even show up there, on certain census records. Yet, almost paradoxically, despite Walter's flaws, he was long-lived, and seems to have had sufficient innate charm to have married twice, and dallied at least once, before his final passing, in 1903.

Walter's first wife, Elizabeth Smith, bore at least four children, Samuel, Catherine, John and Annie, in 1853, 1854, 1856 and 1862 respectively. Records indicate that there was another son, James Allison, born 1874, but this may have been a stepson or even a grandson. There is also some written evidence that Walter was more than friendly with a Catherine Deans. This, however, only lasted a short time, coming to nothing. Elizabeth died in 1879, and he married for a second and final time, in 1882, to a widow by the name of Jane Knox King.

The unsettled childhood homelife, and related poverty are the most likely forces leading to the emigration of three of Walter's children. We'll hear more about them presently, but for now, as promised earlier, we need to take a quick look at one of Walter's younger brothers, also called John.

John Allison was born in 1831. He enlisted in the British Army, probably locally, around 1850. He was stationed in Bermuda in 1854, and it didn't go well. There was nothing wrong with his courage, as he later proved. He just couldn't accept the senselessness of death by fever and disease.

He saw a great many of those around him fall to a variety of unpleasant and fatal fevers. This seems to have been the pressure which led to his desertion. John went over the wall that same year, although it isn't known whether his regiment was still in Bermuda, or had, by that time relocated to Canada. Either way, it is in Canada that we catch our last glimpse of him for some time. He heads into the trees, giving us only one last quick look, over his shoulder. Then he is gone. For four "lost" years. It's 1858 before we see him again, many hundred miles from here.

John's youngest brother, David, was born in 1846. He became an accomplished gardener, working in gardens of increasing complexity, as his skill grew. While still a young bachelor he worked for Lord Abinger at Inverlochy Castle near Fort William. It was while he was employed there, in 1868, that he lost his father, Samuel. He had died, at the age of seventy-six, in the family home at Rosse, Erskine. Samuel's wife, Anne, would, at that time, have been in her mid sixties. She was still a hard-working, vigorous woman, and she was absolutely determined that widowhood was not going to drive her into the Paisley Poorhouse, to be kept by the "charity" of the parochial board.

The next two census returns show that this straight-talking, pipe-smoking matriarch turned her home into a lodging-house, and she was, until just before her eightieth birthday, listed as the lodging-house keeper. Her daughter, Janet, took her in to her home in Glasgow when Anne's health began deteriorating, and she died, aged eighty-one years, at Janet's home, in 1883.

Her son, David, meantime, had married Christina Kilpatrick of Breich, in 1870, at which time he was the gardener at Blackdale, in Largs.

The first of David's children, called Samuel after his grandfather, was born in 1870, in Largs. Janet, known as Jenny, joined the family two years later in 1872. This was the same year in which compulsory schooling was introduced. Alexander, youngest child of the three, made his appearance in 1883. By that time David was Head Gardener with J & P Coats, in Paisley.

James Coats began by creating crepe shawls, and managing his wife's embroidery business. He set up a mill at Ferguslie in 1826, and then retired, in favour of his sons, in 1830. It was these sons, James and Peter, who founded the firm of J & P Coats. They greatly increased the size of the Ferguslie Mill in the 1840's, and opened other mills in Rhode Island, America, at the time of Alexander Allison's birth in 1883.

Further mills were opened up in Russia, Germany, Spain, Hungary, and Austria. By 1890 they had become a major international player, with a capital of almost £6,000,000. They absorbed the famous Clarks' firm in 1896, and if David Allison, working industriously in their gardens, could have glimpsed the future then he would have known that within a century this firm would be one of the largest multinational companies in the world.

David Allison had also become both a Church Officer and a Sunday School Supervisor, by the 1890's. It was convenient, therefore, to rent a house close to the church in question – St James on Underwood Road, in Paisley. The family moved into one of four flats contained in number 3 Underwood Road, and in 1891 their annual rent was £11.10s.

The Mintos remained rooted in the Ravenstruther area throughout the 19th century. Robert began courting while in his teens. He had just turned 20 when he married Rutherford Young from Lanark, in June 1853. His father, James, died when Robert was 25, after which it was fairly easy for Robert to turn his back on the troubled and failing world of the handloom weaver. He had been picking up work as an agricultural worker, and by 1861 he was also working as a railway porter. Four of his ten children had been born by that time. We'll pay particular attention to three of his sons.

With the exception of the first James, (who died aged ten), the eldest surviving son was Henry, followed by Thomas, (my own great grandfather), in 1861. The other six children arrived at fairly regular intervals over the next sixteen years. Second to youngest came George, born in the middle of winter, 1873. He was only sixteen when his father, Robert, so unexpectedly died, following a railway accident, in 1890.

Henry was, by 1891, described as a Ravenstruther Farmer and Fishmonger, wed to Isabella McCallum. They had had seven children by this time, but records show that only four of them were still living in 1891. The other three were already dead, – adding, in their own small way, to Scotland's shame, in the closing years of the 19th century. Scottish infant mortality rates had climbed to their highest point in history.

The political reforms, and agricultural and industrial improvements of the last hundred years had done nothing to alleviate the problems of bad housing and poor public health. (In the 1890's the average number of infants dying before their first birthday – per thousand live births – was 130). Economic and social reform, and some sustained investment would have begun the process of lowering the numbers of infant deaths, but these improvements were still some years in the future.

It is said that "time heals", and the dark times did pass for Henry and Isabella. They went on to add a further five children to their surviving four by 1903, and we'll hear more about some of them, and their families, as the next century unfolds.

Henry's brother, Thomas was, by the age of twenty four, a letter sorter, working in Edinburgh. He had married "the girl from next door", in June 1885, in Carstairs. This was Joan Watson Sinclair, who, like Thomas, was also from Ravenstruther. They lived in Downfield Place in Edinburgh, and had a son, whom they named Robert, in mid-November 1887, but sadly Joan passed away eighteen days later of post-natal complications, on the 1st December.

Two years later, when Thomas married Mary Hamilton, on 1st August 1890, he was described as a Post Office Clerk. He and Mary continued to live in Edinburgh, where both of their daughters, Mary and Rutherford, were born, in 1891, and 1894 respectively. Before long,

Thomas secured further advancement within the Post Office, accepting the position of Postmaster at Maybole in Ayrshire.

And George, Thomas's younger brother? He got married, just as the century was winding itself towards a close. The 24th June 1897 was the day that he exchanged marriage vows with his beloved Agnes Walker. They were married at her home, Sawmill Cottage, in Granton, north of Edinburgh. It was only three days after the summer solstice, and the nights were light. There was peace in the world, and a sense of anticipation. People were beginning to ask that question . . . "What would the next century bring?"

Table Three, on page 84, summarises Minto and Allison genealogies through the 19th century, and also cross-references tables of 20th century descendants on later pages.

Chapter Four

Heavy Turbulence

*"A well-written life is almost as
rare as a well-spent one."*
Thomas Carlyle

The turn of the century, and the beginning of the Edwardian Era, brought big changes, of a variety of different kinds. Wealthy people saw improvements in comfort and standards of living. There were national celebrations to mark the return of the troops from the Boer War. In Glasgow, the two "Great Exhibitions" were held in 1901, and 1911, and together pretty much bracketed the Edwardian Period.

The majority of the Scottish people didn't see any improvement in their conditions during this time however. There was mass overcrowding in the urban areas. This led to a number of related problems such as continued high infant mortality, epidemic levels of tuberculosis, sewage in the drinking wells, toxic waste contamination, and simple, but deadly malnutrition.

The widespread nature of these problems served to accelerate social change across the country. Keir Hardie's Independent Labour Party became the Labour Party in 1906. Salaries for MP's, which had first been proposed by those Chartists, so long before, were introduced in 1911, opening the door for anyone to stand for Parliament. The Co-operative movement was also developing fast at this time.

Trade Unions gained strength and influence in this period – this was the time of John MacLean, Red Clydesider, and hero of many a folk ballad. A Glasgow schoolmaster, John was a committed Communist, joining the Social Democratic Federation in 1903. He campaigned for Scottish socialism, and Trade Unions rights guaranteed by legislation.

These years prior to 1914 were therefore years of change, and of unrest. They were also years which saw the Mintos and the Allisons moving ever closer to the point of impact. And yet there was still much that would happen to each family first.

Only one of David Allison's three children survived beyond the end of 1913. Janet died suddenly in 1907 at the age of 35. Sam was a travelling joiner, who had worked in both Spain and Madeira, before becoming incapacitated by poor health. He suffered from kidney disease, and became ever less mobile. One unusual consequence of his condition was that, while bored and housebound, Sam became increasingly interested in the stockmarket, and was ultimately reasonably successful.

Sadly, he finally succumbed to his illness in 1913, dying, aged 42. His legacy made it possible for his parents to move from their rented accommodation in Underwood Road, to their own house, called Woodcliff, in Elderslie (see next page). Alexander, 13 years younger than Sam, was at this time working as a Maths teacher in Lanark Grammar School.

By contrast, most of Robert Minto's offspring were long lived. Henry, the eldest surviving son, was having an expensive time, in that first decade. It was two of his daughters, Isabella and Margaret, who chose to marry the Plenderleith brothers (see page 34). The summers of both 1908 and 1909 were therefore times of family celebration. Big families mean big weddings, so the festivities were enjoyed by many Mintos and Plenderleiths. Among the many siblings who toasted their sisters' future happiness was Henry and Isabella's eldest surviving son Robert.

Henry's younger brother Thomas was still working for the Post Office, although no longer in Ayrshire. Maybole had proven to be a temporary stop-over, and on 19th February 1904 he left there to become Postmaster in Blairgowrie.

Thomas' daughters continued their education at Blairgowrie, and were at University within what seemed to be just a few short years. The youngest, Rutherford (called Ruth), was studying for an MA at Saint Andrews University.

Woodcliff, Elderslie, (circa 1920).

Woodcliff, Elderslie, (2003).

Presentation (upon leaving Maybole). Inscription :

Presented to Mr & Mrs Minto by the staff of Maybole Post Office and sub-offices on the occasion of their leaving for Blairgowrie, 19th February, 1904.

Schooldays at Blairgowrie about 1906
(Ruth Minto – third from left, front row).

George Minto, second to youngest of Robert's brood, was a master blacksmith, wheelwright, and farrier in Braidwood. It had been a good trade, in a beautiful area. But the world was changing, and demand for traditional skills and crafts was falling. At the same time, the number of sons that George had was growing. The arithmetic was simple, and George decided that leaving was the answer. He left London, for Australia, on 3rd February 1911 aboard "RMS Otway", an Orient Line steamer.

We'll hear much more, about George, and the family descending from his five boys, in coming chapters. For now, however, we will rejoin George's elder brother Thomas, his wife Mary, and their family, in Scotland.

Stormclouds were gathering in the world, at large. The Austrian heir-presumptive, Franz Ferdinand had been killed by Bosnian terrorists at Sarajevo, on 28th June 1914. War was just around the corner.

Thomas's daughters, Mary and Ruth, were in France on holiday, at the outbreak of the First World War. Ruth had just turned twenty years old, some two weeks earlier, before they left for France. Her diary, of their thoughts and actions during this critical period, has never before been published. I have included abridged excerpts of that diary here, as it contains valuable first-hand insights, into both Ruth's thinking, and also the actual description of events as they unfolded, in France.

There is an added poignancy, and an edge, to this "well-written life", when we realise that the conflict is going to take Ruth's elder half-brother, Robert, on the 19th June 1917. He is buried near Popperinge in France. Her only other sibling, Mary, who was with her during the writing of this diary, will be taken by the influenza epidemic, on 13th October 1918.

From Ruth Minto's diary – kept in France, 30th July to 10th August 1914 :

We left Edinburgh on Thursday morning, 30th July, en route for London, Southampton and St Malo. By "we" I mean two of us, my sister, (Mary), and myself.

Our journey to London was uneventful. We arrived there about 4.30pm and spent the hours between that and 10.30pm, (when the boat train left Waterloo Station for Southampton), mainly eating and sight-seeing from the tops of buses.

It seems rather amusing now to look back on that outward journey when our sole thought was whether the luggage should be registered or not, and supposing we got aboard the wrong boat at Southampton docks at 12 o' clock that night, what would happen?

However, we reached Southampton at midnight. Next morning about 11 o' clock saw us approaching the coast of Brittany. Our first view of St Malo was certainly imposing. The town is a very perfect survival of days of the middle ages, when all continental towns were ringed round for protection by massive walls and towers. These, in the case of St Malo, rise from the sea to a considerable height, and the breadth is such that two people can walk abreast with ease, along the tops.

We arrive without mishap at the villa St Alice, where we mean to stay for the month. There was a goodly company of us in the Boarding House, mostly English, but as most of them departed soon after, I shall mention only these – a nurse, an English lady who knew little French, a French lady from Paris who knew no English, and an indispensable Welshman who was the only male in the establishment.

We had lunch when we arrived and Mlle Andrew from Paris immediately asked us "Well, what about the war" . We thought we had misunderstood her Parisien accent, but no, she repeated her question. War! What war was there? Then we suggested the Austria/Serbian war – she was impatient and rather annoyed when we told her that we had heard nothing of the German menace in England.

We dismissed the incident from our minds but the next day, Saturday, it was rather dramatically resurrected. Our boarding house was about a mile out from St Malo, in one of it's suburbs, St Servain. We had decided to walk in and view St Malo. Nearing the town, which is entered by four gates, we saw a number of excited people in the square, just inside the main gates. They were straining their eyes in our direction, and looking back we saw several cyclists in a neck to neck race. As they approached we noticed that they carried newspapers, and the crowd at once pounced on them. We finally succeeded in getting one. It was a single sheet but it's contents were stupendous, for there we saw the headline "German concentration on the French frontier, and the violation of Luxembourg neutrality". Not till then did we realise what awful import lay behind the words, and I am not sure that we sensed it even them.

We went into a Patisserie to talk things out over a cup of tea, and there, while we were seated, we heard a solemn peal ring out and then again and again. We did not understand it, but it's message, for it's people, was plain.

The streets of St Malo are old, cobbled and narrow, and within the space of twenty minutes time they seemed overflowing with people. Here were men shaking hands with their friends and giving the right or left or whichever lay nearest. It is the French token of farewell. There were women silently endeavouring to master their grief.

Greatly wondering, we followed the stream and found ourselves opposite the Mairie or Town Hall, outside the door of which was posted the mobilisation order for the French army.

On the road we met groups of soldiers in twos and threes, clattering down to the Mairie to report, picturesque in their red felt trousers and big blue overcoats, reaching to the knee and looped back in front. Some carried their extra pair of boots round their neck.

I do not know how the news of the war was received in England . . . I do know of the terrible depression that reigned in this corner of France. Everyone wept, not hysterically, but hopelessly and despairingly, and Mlle Gouarne whispered that we, being an insular people, could not understand it, but that if this war ended like that of 1870, (which she remembered),

France, her Motherland, would be a German Province.

Mlle Andrew was greatly excited and someone, mote for something to say than anything else, suggested that perhaps after all, there might be no war. Never shall I forget her reply. "Pas de guerre betisse – voila les Francaise, voila les Allemands comme des chats prêt a elancer".

Next day being Sunday, Mlle Gouarne explained that we must go down to the Mairie and register ourselves at once, as all the Germans had been ordered to leave before six next morning.

When we got down, we found several farmers giving details as to their stock of cattle, etc., and were very kindly received by the Mayor and a dapper little man in Knicker-bockers and shirt sleeves, whose status and name we never determined but with whom we afterwards struck up a friendship, always referring to him as our friend with the twinkle because of the following incident. When the Welshman was asked his nationality, instead of replying Anglais, he answered "Pays de Gael". When our turn came we answered Ecossais. The little man looked at us intently, then his face lit up, his eyes twinkled and he smiled. "Ah oui" he said, "Scotch Whisky". These were the only English words he knew.

Tuesday, after dinner, accompanied by the indispensable Williams, we set out for St Malo. When we arrived at the square at the entrance to the Barracks, which is bordered on one side by Restaurants, we found an animated throng – soldiers, civilians, wine, women, and song – all in abundance. We sat down at one of the little tables in the square and ordered a liqueur. The band struck up first the Marseillaise, we rose and clinked glasses, then God Save the King, then the Russian National Anthem and so on. Each time we rose, each time we clinked glasses, and the crowd cried itself hoarse – "Vive La France, Vive l'Armee, Vive l'Entente Cordiale".

Afterwards we walked up to the walls and along the battlements. Across the Rance, the lights of Dinard were twinkling like precious stones in the dark, gleaming, expanse of *the sea. The night was calm and, save for the occasional burst of cheering brought to us from below, was very silent. Our thoughts were very mixed but little did we realise that at that very moment the British nation was sitting in council debating whether to take the path of shameful ease or vindicate it's sacred international obligations by it's life blood and the sword.*

On Wednesday morning when we went out, we were greeted with smiles, and when we reached the Mairie, where the only news we got was displayed on blackboards, (for newspapers were practically unknown), we saw that on Tuesday at midnight England had declared war on Germany. A strange exultation possessed us and when the Mayor came up and solemnly shook hands with us saying "Vive l'Angleterre" we both felt rather choky.

In the evening we went down to the mouth of the river Rance. The promise of the day was fulfilled in the night. A big, calm moon sailed thro' the sky and lit up the waters of the river and the Rock, on which stands a figure of the Virgin all silvered over. She is casting her protective arms over the waters and fishermen of Brittany. We stood on a hill; round us, the houses looked white and bright, most of them nestling in the dark shadows of trees. On the way back we met a weary French soldier tramping heavily along. "Vive l'Armee" we cried, and he brought his heels together with a click. "Voutes etes gentils mes amis, Vive l'Armee".

Next day we got a telegram with a peremptory message to return at once, and I don't know if we felt exactly sorry. However, the English boat had already sailed that day, so we had to wait until Friday.

So Friday was spent packing and arranging to go back. Our boat was due to sail at 6pm, and at about 5pm, as we were preparing to depart, up the stairs came Mlle, with a voice of tragedy. "You cannot go", she cried. "There is no English boat". We gaped, and then we laughed, and then wished we hadn't. "Why", we asked. She shrugged her shoulders. "They say the

Germans have mined the Channel and an English ship has already been sunk". (This, afterwards, we discovered, was the Amphion). It was a blue look out. Off we hurried to the boat's offices in St Malo, meeting, on the way, practically every other English person in the town.

There they had no information, but the clerk told us, after we had worried him sufficiently, that probably the Company's boats had been requisitioned, as transports for an expeditionary force. That was certainly a relief from the other idea and seemed reasonable enough. But what about another boat? He did not know. Sadly, we went back. Two days before, we had refused to return. Now that we could not get, we were longing to go.

We were not a merry party that night. On Saturday we went down to see if our twinkly friend in the knickerbockers and short sleeves knew anything. He did not, but he assured us that he would find something to amuse us if we assisted him to write the news on the blackboards and carry them out, which we did. Then he explained his idea – why not go over to the College of Priests and assist in sewing and altering the uniforms of the reservists? Seeing us look doubtful, he hastily added that the sewing would consist of sewing on the regimental numbers to the vest and kepi. Well, that did not sound ambitious, so off we went.

We were ushered into a huge, bare hall. Women were busy shortening jackets and trousers, sewing on buttons, etc. To my great dismay I was presented with a pair of trousers and requested to shorten them. It was useless to argue that I had come to sew on numbers and could not shorten trousers, so after much cogitation the thing was simply done by cutting bits off the legs and sewing the seams up again. Nurse Taylor did one leg. I did the other, and afterwards we had qualms as to whether one was not shorter than it's neighbour. However the soldier was very polite and assured us that it really did not matter at all.

Sunday 9th August was a beautiful day. The sun was brilliant, the shade of the fig-tree in the garden was most inviting, and we were surrounded by friendly people. Having decided to unpack *and make the best of things, Fate then played us a scurvy trick. There was a violent peal at the gate-bell and a messenger from the shipping company arrived to say that a boat was coming into port that night which would take us to Jersey, where we would be picked up by another boat – some time. All English people were recommended to go.*

Our goodbyes at the Pension are most embarrassing, but we finally get down to the pier. An hour passes – then another hour, and still no sign of a boat. Then we hear a cheer. She has been sighted from the Ramparts. Our spirits revive. Meanwhile all St Malo is on the pier. Throngs of soldats in their baggy uniforms, dapper officers in blue vests and red, black-braided breeches, smiling Breton maids in Sunday garb, voluminous skirts and huge white coifs.

Never shall I forget that scene – it was now near nine o'clock and the light was failing. We embarked at once, then we sang Marseillaise, then Rule Brittania, then God Save the King, then the Marseillaise again, and always in between were cries of Vive la France, Vive l'Angleterre, Vive l'Entente Cordiale. We were all on deck, perched on every available eminence, and as the boat prepared to cast off, cheer after cheer arose from the soldiers, answered heartily from the deck. Then the boat steams out, turns, and we have our last glimpse – a half light, a grey pier splashed with red and blue, and kindly and simple folks beside themselves with emotion.

That picture I shall always retain, (even though the war has now become a harrowing reality), as symbolic of our union with a brave people, in an attempt to crush an unscrupulous tyrant.

The next four years were a curse upon the world, an affliction that took the youth of many nations. All four of my grandparents survived it, but between them they lost six siblings over the four year period.

Robert Minto had a grandson called Robert Minto in each of five different branches of the family. All five of these Robert Mintos were born between 1884 and 1898, and all five fought in the First World War. Two of them died there.

Robert, son of Henry, who had been toasting his sister's marriage nine years earlier, was killed in action on 23rd April 1917. Lacking a grave, his name appears on the Arras Memorial. His cousin, Robert, son of Thomas, was also killed in action, as we have heard, in June 1917. Their uncle George had also returned from Australia to fight in the war. He served in France with the Australian Imperial Forces. He too was tragically killed in action, on 23rd September 1917. He is buried near his nephew, (Thomas's boy), at Popperinge.

The Arras Memorial.

The stones in those French cemeteries seem as numerous as grains of sand upon a foreign shore, and yet, like some vast catalogue, each stone is the door to a tale like this one. They represent a lost generation, and almost every household in the land will forever have empty places, the shape of the unborn descendants of those who fell.

Alexander Allison served with the Cameronians, as a 2nd Lieutenant in the Scottish Rifles from 1914 until 1919. He saw service with a vengeance in France. He was wounded by an enemy shell in 1916, and was sent home for weeks, to convalesce. He returned to the front, and was wounded again in 1917. This time he was shot in the chest and in the arm. His convalescence was longer second time, but he eventually returned to the front, later that year. For the rest of the war he worked with the Observer Corps, from a foxhole, far in front of the lines, drawing enemy positions and troop movements on a pad, and no doubt drawing heavy enemy fire as well.

After the war was over, Alexander was retained on the Front, leading a clean-up squad that cleared the land of the debris of war, and again made it safe for everyday life. It was with considerable relief that his father, David, welcomed this, his last surviving child, home safely, to Elderslie, in early 1919.

Post-war Scotland was no Eden. World trade began a heavy downturn in 1919, and Scotland suffered more than the rest of Britain. Jobs were scarce, new industries were cautious of commitment, due to the "Red Clydeside" image, Many ex-servicemen had cause to wonder what the future held, as they stared unemployment in the face.

A teaching qualification was a boon, and so, luckily, within weeks Alexander was back in Lanark, firstly in a temporary post – as acting head of New Lanark School, and then, in September, as Science and Botany teacher at Lanark Grammar.

There he got to know young Ruth Minto, the English teacher, and diary writer. I have it on good authority, and by first-hand account, that many of the girls in the school watched intently, as romance burgeoned between these, the popular Miss, and the returned war hero.

After all the centuries that we've been watching these families circling closer, at least it wasn't an over-long courtship. They were married in Edinburgh, Canongate, on 2nd August, 1921. They had both lost all of their siblings over the preceding fourteen years, but at least they had found each other. They set up home in Lanark, and with no premonition of the tragedy yet to come, excitedly awaited what the rest of the twentieth century had to show them.

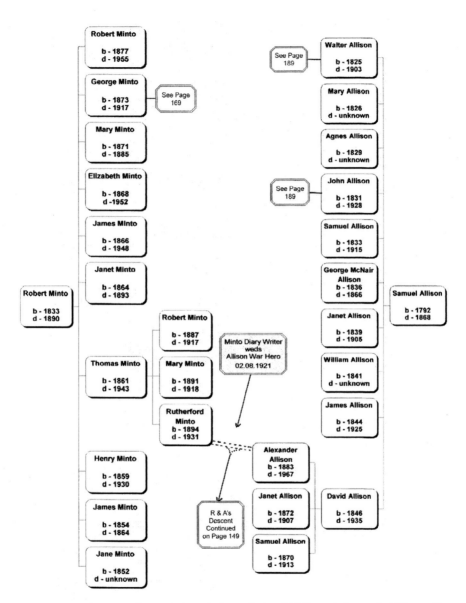

Mintos and Allisons – from Robert Minto (born 1833) and Samuel Allison (born 1792), through to the marriage of their grandchildren, Rutherford Minto and Alexander Allison, in 1921.

Chapter Five

To the Farthest Reaches of the World

*"The waves have some mercy, but
the rocks have no mercy at all."*
From the Gaelic

We've met George Minto several times before. We've seen the big pieces that make up the shape of his life. As a tiny baby, he cried, as the snow piled up outside, and his mother, Rutherford, rocked and soothed him through that first deep winter of 1873 into 1874.

His father, Robert, although previously a railway worker, was, through the years of George's growing, an agricultural labourer. The precious evening times spent talking with his father, by the fire, both in Ravenstruther and elsewhere, fueled his curiosity about rural skills and farming, and sparked an interest in blacksmithing.

Robert was suddenly taken from him in 1890, dying of a cranial sepsis, following a railway accident. Although only sixteen, that was more than amply old enough for him to understand the irony of a railway accident causing his father's death years after Robert had ceased to be a railway worker.

By 1891 George had moved a few doors down the road in Ravenstruther. He had become a boarder with John Lyon the local blacksmith, and was working hard at a blacksmithing apprenticeship. Upon completing his time at John's smithy, he then moved to Edinburgh, to take up a position as farrier, in a smithy there.

By the age of twenty three George had met and married Agnes Walker, (great grand-daughter of a John Walker, who had been factor to the Duke of Roxburgh). Their marriage took place, as we have read, in 1897, and they set up home first in Edinburgh, and later in Braidwood, where George plied his trade as blacksmith, farrier, and wheelwright.

We have heard, too, of how rural Lanarkshire was a favoured location for such an endeavour. As well as being reasonably close to all of his other family members, the area was still predominantly agricultural. It was also an attractive area in which to live and work.

The changing social and economic situation within the country inevitably took its toll, however, and by 1911 George and Agnes had decided to take their ever-growing tribe of boys, and seek a better-founded life in Australia. They travelled on the RMS Otway, and made landfall in Brisbane on 20th March 1911.

When the First World War broke out, George felt compelled to join up, with the Australian Imperial forces, in order to return to Europe, and stand with those from his home, against the forces of German aggression. This was both heroic, and tragic. He was killed on 23rd September 1917, at the age of 43, near Ypres, and lies now in the Nine Elms British Cemetery in Poperinge, in Belgium.

Is this enough for you? It may indeed be enough for some people, who are travelling through here, at speed. But it isn't half enough for in-depth insight. The big pieces in any life can be covered in just a page or two. What are these pieces though, without the mortar that holds them in place. They are nought but a tumbled heap of fragments on the ground. To see the stunning mosaic that is a life, (any life), in it's full grandeur, we need to be aware of the background upon which the larger pieces rest. And this life, in particular, is of great interest, as, when it comes to Rivers Running Far, none ended up farther from the source than George.

So how have he and Agnes got on, since their happy union in June, 1897. (As first mentioned on page 70). Where have they lived? What has their life been like, first in Edinburgh, and then beyond?

George and Agnes were well-blessed with children. Their firstborn was Robert, born in Edinburgh on 1st August, 1898. By the time he was joined by a little brother, George, in June almost two years later, it was already the twentieth century.

By this time George (senior) had been working in Granton, Edinburgh for years. He had done well and was recognised as a master blacksmith. He and Agnes felt that it was time for him to set up his own Smithy, and, after some searching, they found the very place.

Whinnyknowe Smithy, Harestanes was located at the crossroads in Braidwood, on the west side of the Lanark to Carluke Road, and the south side of the Crossford road. Here George developed both home and workplace.

The forge was the living, burning, heart of his family's world. Here, he practiced, as one of the holders of the secrets of the "Iron Lords"- those fierce Celts so successful in the earlier landscape. And these secrets have, of course, been bolstered by the added expertise of a further two millennia working the metal.

By the early years of the twentieth century the hot fire was kept going by a forced draught, created by the bellows, but carried, through a cast-iron object, (known as a tuyere), to the base of the fire. Here, the air flow increased the temperature of the fire to a white-hot glare, in almost no time, thus heating the iron faster, with less use of coal.

The Whinnyknowe hammers clanged like mysterious bells on the anvil, and sparks often flew, near the glowing fire. George always made sure that the "slack tub", near the flames, was full of water, to cool the exuberance of the hot iron. The water in the tub was also useful for occasionally sprinkling out on the "clinker" – (the stony residue from the burnt coals), on the workshop floor, to prevent the place from catching alight.

It's no wonder that there are so many stories about Smithing, in mythology. The Dwarven smiths of the Norse, Vulcan the god of the Greeks, and Wayland Smith of English legend, are all portrayed as magical beings, possessed of special powers. This picture is understandable, when we think of the mysterious fire, worked upon, and bent to the smith's will. And at the other end of the process, the wonder of creation, resulting in all manner of metal objects that all manner of people required or desired, whether those customers were landed gentry, farmers, merchants, tradesmen, or housewives.

The smithy was a treasure-house of utensils for all – ploughs, sickles, scythes, horse harness, ox-yoke, nuts and bolts, axes, shovels, fire-irons, wedges, hinges, chains, hoes, forks, decorative railing, and even weathercocks – whether it was hardware or tools, for home or work, it all took shape in the fire.

Amongst the many items created in George's fire were horseshoes. This was because, as well as being a master blacksmith, he was also a farrier, which, put quite simply, is a smith who shoes horses.

The Braidwood smithy and house, circa 1904.

George believed in the maxim that "the more strings a man has to his bow, the more financially secure he is", and as an accomplished craftsman he applied that maxim by adding wheelwright to his existing expertise as smith and farrier.

The wheelwright used in-depth knowledge of the properties of timber to create wagons which would give years of useful service. The woods of rural Lanarkshire provided the materials for George to buy, for use in different parts of the construction.

There was a distinct annual rhythm to this, with oak purchased spring and early summer, and ash, elm and beech in the middle of winter. All of these various woods were then seasoned for perhaps five or six years before reaching the workbench, and building actually beginning.

The wheels were the hardest part of any wagon-construction, hence the profession being called wheelwright, and not wagon-maker. A whole wagon could take six months to build, but each of the completed wheels was individually capable of carrying three-quarters of a ton. Altogether, then, the finished article was a formidable creation, once horsepower was added.

A Master of the Forge was often also blessed with a talent for innovation, and George was no exception. In fact he applied to the Patent Office on 3rd February 1906 describing his acclaimed new invention, the improved horseshoe. He appended one sheet of drawings, (next page), and some text explaining the considerable benefits that such an innovation would bring. The patent was accepted on 4th October 1906, with no single hint of the disturbance it was later to create.

George's boys were increasingly helpful around the smithy, as they grew older. By 1907, Robert and George had been joined by Henry, Adam, and Thomas, and so the house was rarely quiet.

Once they reached the age of five they went to Braidwood school, from 9am to 4pm, Monday to Friday. It was a walk of less than a mile, downhill through the woods, towards Crossford on the River Clyde. Just beyond the School, on the road to the river, the boys were fascinated by the tall and mysterious keep of Hallbar Tower. This was the best preserved 15th century Tower-House in Lanarkshire, having been renovated in both 1581 and 1861. Even today its walls are over 5 feet thick, and a flagstone roof caps the pigeon loft.

Despite the allure of ancient castles, however, the boys were fairly self-disciplined about heading straight to school in the morning. Coming back was not always as straightforward, as spirits would be running high, and the surrounding woods and fields represented an irresistible playground.

Some days, though, they would hurry, if they knew that their father, George, was fixing some local lad's bicycle. They found this particular task both fascinating, and useful, and probably worth learning for themselves.

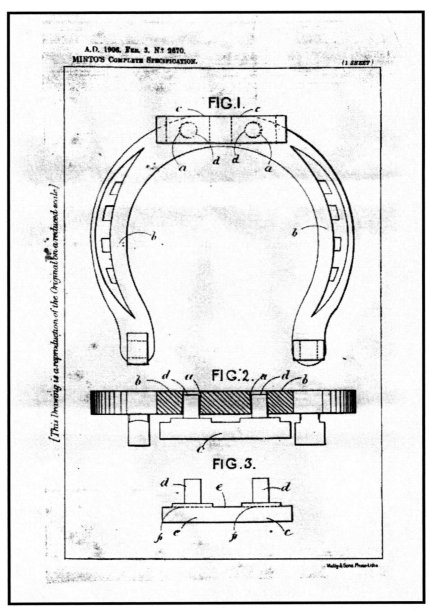

Improvements in, and relating to, Horse Shoes –
No 2670 (Accepted 4th October, 1906).

Winter, too, would be a reason for hurrying home, and not just because of the early dark. During cold snaps nearby Braidwood Loch would freeze over, and then the sport would begin. Favourite among all the games that they played would be when their father, George, joined them, skating around on the ice, with one son holding tightly to each end of his long scarf, which he tied around his waist, in the style of a human maypole.

In 1909 there were disquieting developments in the world of horseshoe production, which cast a bit of a pall on the day to day life of the family. A large metalworking firm in Newcastle-upon-Tyne began producing the Minto horseshoe, without permission. Family hearsay reports that, as patent-holders, George and Agnes took this firm to court, and won their case. Later, however, the same firm decided to contest the ruling, and by 1910, George was beginning to worry about whether his finances could withstand this latest threat, or indeed whether there might just be a simpler answer elsewhere. He decided to talk it over with family.

The Braidwood Mintos still had close links with their Ravenstruther relatives, and the boys would regularly pile high the family horse-and-trap for an expedition to see their Grandmother there. And at times like these she was always a sympathetic ear, where George could blether about the problems looming up ahead.

It was on one of the last of these trips that Adam ended up in disgrace. All boys fight, and argue, especially brothers. That's probably axiomatic. Still, even Adam admitted that, angry or not, it was possibly unwise of him to lock his elder brother, Henry, in the privy (outside toilet), just before they left for home. It was some considerable time before anyone noticed that one of the boys was missing, at which point the horse, Daisy, was turned around. It wasn't long until they met their cousins pedalling furiously towards them, from the opposite direction, with Henry mounted on the handlebars of one of the bikes. He had finally been discovered where his five-year old gaoler had left him – imprisoned in the lavatory!

The smithy had provided a good living for them. Braidwood was a great place for the boys to grow and play, and George was a liked and respected member of the community.

Maggie Waddell (nee Gray), a farmer's daughter born near Carluke in 1902, said that "As a child, she thought that the smithy was the warmest place in Scotland". She also commented that the smithy worked long hours as it was lit well into the night. But sometimes even the most well-settled of lives can become subject to the external force described on page 40 – the "Push" that brings unwelcome change.

Although George was a skilled smith, farrier and wright, this had not provided the security that he had expected. The unthinkable was happening right before his eyes. Agnes was supportive, reassuring him, and telling him that it wasn't his fault. That no-one could have seen it coming. Just imagine – the end of "the Age of the Horse". How unlikely was that, even just ten years earlier.

And she was right. The development and spread of the motor car had, in historical terms, happened with shocking speed. In 1886 Karl Benz patented the first practical internal combustion automobile. In 1894 Frank and Charles Duryea formed the first American company to produce gasoline cars, and in 1901 the Oldsmobile Curved Dash Runabout from Michigan became the first mass-produced car. It's price tag was $650 dollars, and 425 were produced. 1908 was probably the real death knell for the Age of the Horse, however. This was the year that Henry Ford's $850 Model T made its first appearance.

Unfortunately, horse-related work formed the core of all the services that George offered. The greatest portion of his business came from the agricultural sector, providing and repairing everything from agricultural implements to wagons. But this was by no means the whole sum of his work. There were the carriages and mounts of the wealthy to service, and the many requirements of the local trades.

The decline of horsepower, the coming of the car, and the rise in mechanisation and mass-production, in everything from tool-making to garden gates, signalled the end of the blacksmith's position in the heart of the community. It signalled increasingly difficult times ahead, too, for the financial welfare of George and his family.

When emigration had first been mentioned earlier, it was mostly as a joke or passing aside. As things continued to change, and also in the face of further legal wrangles over the whole Horseshoe patent situation, things became swiftly more serious. Then they became aware of the government assisted scheme to encourage farmers to emigrate to Australia.

George's father, Robert, had been an agricultural worker. This, together with knowledge gained while smithing for agricultural customers, gave George enough expertise to feel comfortable describing himself as "farmer". One thing was sure in that fast-changing world; that there was no assistance on offer for blacksmiths. It became a topic of more frequent discussion between George and Agnes, through the months of 1910.

When decision-time finally came round, the choice wasn't so hard. The promise was a new life with the likelihood of considerably greater financial stability, not just for himself and Agnes, but also for his boys. Against this, to be sure, there was the pain and distress of parting with their families. As parents, however, came the necessity to provide for their young, as best they could.

The Mintos just prior to emigration, 1911.

The paperwork was completed towards the end of 1910, and thus the Mintos of Braidwood prepared to spend their last Christmas in Scotland. After New Year had passed, arrangements stepped up a gear, and they began packing the big cabin trunk with all the essentials for their new life.

This was probably the period when the "Pull" began taking over from the "Push", as the excitement began to build, and the family started to lean forward towards their departure date. That "big step" away from solid ground began with the journey to London, and embarkation on the RMS Otway, a new Orient Line steamer.

The Otway was a large twin-screw vessel of 12000 tons register, which had only been launched two years before. There was accommodation for 280 in first class, 130 in second class, and 900 in third class. In addition, there were also 350 crew.

The ship was full to overflowing. Full both with emigrants like themselves, taking the "big step", and also full of emotions running high. The decks positively thrummed with the feelings of those aboard. The anticipation of a new start, the dread of the great unknown, the determination to make a go of it, the heart's keening lament at the leaving of loved ones forever, and the simple excitement of the children at the prospect of such an adventure.

After leaving the Thames estuary on 3rd February 1911, the days passed, sliding one into the next, with the same ease with which the Otway sailed ever southwards. Passenger numbers created a community which resembled the population of a small rural village. It wasn't long, especially under the cramped conditions, until they began to get to know one another. Shipboard activities, such as organised foot-races around the deck, helped everyone to integrate.

As well as paying for passage, and feeling the raw bite of homesickness, they all had something else in common too. It was Mrs Mary Ann Manbey who pointed out this other expense to Agnes Minto, shortly after the ship crossed the equator. The other cost of this voyage was the permanent loss of one summer. They were beating ever further south, and although it was only the beginning of March, autumn had already begun in the southern hemisphere.

The Manbeys became shipboard friends during the voyage, and they were also a welcome distraction when it came to amusing the boys, as the monotony of the voyage began to grate. They were good company, but Brisbane, unfortunately, was not the end of their journey. They were to transfer, along with 3 others, to the coastal steamer, Yongala, for onward travel to Townsville.

It was a source of wonder, and more than a little irritation, to the younger boys, that even after seeing the western coast, smelling the gum trees, and arriving at Fremantle, their journey had yet another two weeks to go. After all, weren't they now in Australia?

As landfall in Brisbane drew ever closer, those passengers who were travelling onwards grew more uneasy. The Otway was running a little behind schedule, and there was always the worry that they would miss their connection and be stranded in Brisbane. Some even chose to pray that their connection be made. George and Agnes tried to reassure them that everything would work out, and sure enough, the last couple of days were covered at the Otway's full speed of 18 knots. She made up time and berthed on 20th March 1911.

The city's newspaper, the Brisbane Courier, reported that: "RMS "Otway" docked at Pinkenba. The new Queenslanders were met on behalf of the Immigration Department by Mr K.A. Schulz, who took them under his charge, and had them and their belongings conveyed up the river to the Immigration Depot, Kangaroo Point, by the tender Boko".

The Yongala wasn't due to leave until the following day. There was plenty of time, therefore, for the Mintos to wish the Manbeys well, while all necessary arrangements were being made for the next leg of the Manbeys' voyage. During this period almost 700 tons of cargo was being loaded, together with the Yongala's most unusual passenger – a horse called Moonshine, which was eagerly awaited in Townsville. The Yongala left Brisbane just slightly behind schedule, and headed north for Townsville and Cairns, stopping briefly in Mackay on 23rd March, to drop off and receive passengers, and to deliver some cargo.

By 1.40pm she was on her way again, with 124 people aboard. She hadn't yet slipped below the horizon when the signal station at Mackay received notification of a cyclone in the Townsville/Mackay vicinity. The Yongala, unfortunately, was not one of the few ships that carried a radio, in 1911.

In the early evening the lighthouse keeper on Dent Island saw her sail past, towards the rising storm. It was the last that anyone saw of the doomed steamer or any of the people aboard her. She was declared missing on the 26th March , and was the subject of a Marine Board of Queensland inquiry in June 1911. After much deliberation, this inquiry – "with no desire to indulge in idle speculation, simply found that after becoming lost to view by the light keeper at Dent Island, the fate of the Yongala passed beyond human ken into the realms of conjecture, to add one more to the mysteries of the sea".

There was no trace of the people who sailed on the Yongala, and the only body ever found was that of the racehorse, Moonshine, washed ashore at the mouth of Gordon Creek not far from Townsville.

The world had to wait until 1958 to learn the fate of the unfortunate vessel. George Konrat, a salvage and construction diver from Cairns, dived some twelve nautical miles east of Cape Bowling Green, on a 300 foot long wreck that he later identified as the Yongala by the lettering of the name on the bow.

In this case it was the unforgiving waters of the sea which took the ship, and not the rocks that the old Gaelic proverb warn against – "The waves have some mercy, but the rocks have no mercy at all." She went down in about 80 feet of water, hammered under, by mountains of solid water flooding over the bows and onto the foredecks. Waves with no mercy.

We will never know whether she just went straight to the bottom through sheer weight of water, or whether she tried, in vain, to escape her fate, and capsized while trying to turn. What we do know, by the lack of any of the ship's life-saving equipment being used, is that the end came shockingly fast, and when the Yongala foundered, she went down like a stone.

It took the Mintos time to get over the shockwave caused by the disappearance of the Yongala and the loss of all aboard. Despite this, though, all the sights and sounds and smells of this new continent quite overwhelmed them, and it wasn't long until they started to really look around, and then began settling in, to this, their new home.

Brisbane, in 1911, was a city of almost 80,000 people. It boasted gas lighting, piped water, and a University offering the Commonwealth State of Queensland courses in Arts, Sciences and Engineering. All this was a far cry from it's humble beginnings as a penal colony.

The city itself stood atop cliff-faced bluffs on both banks of the river, but with the main business centre lying to the north of the waterway. The buildings were all low level, and, due to this, the city sprawled miles out into the country. As in Rome, the dwellings were built on many hills, and the developers had cleared large areas of bush in order to construct new streets.

In the world of Homer's classical literature, Ithaca, in Greece, was truly a magical place, and stood for the homecoming. Odysseus sailed for a decade to reach this, his home, and many sailors quote Ithaca as the ultimate goal. It is therefore fitting and appropriate that George and Agnes, too, found an end to their journeying in a suburb called Ithaca. This area had a strong Scottish and Irish immigrant community. The churches which served these peoples were, of course, mainly Presbyterian, Methodist, and Roman Catholic. The Mintos would, at first, have attended the Ithaca Presbyterian Church, which can still be seen today, behind the newer building, which was opened seventy-five years ago.

Many homes at that time were variations on the "Queenslander" – a timberboard house with wrap-round verandas, many doors, and with much of the accommodation provided on the first floor. This design was a response to the overwhelming heat of a Queensland summer, providing through-draughts, and shaded, yet outdoor seating.

After an initial period renting in the area, George and Agnes chose to build, in School Street. Their house, (finished in 1914, and called Braidwood), was one of only two on the street at that time. It was around this period that it was decided to rename the road as Lugg Street, after Alderman Lugg. In the spirit of economy the new name was merely stuck up on top of the old signpost. But boys being boys, (and Minto boys at that), it "slipped", and the fingerboard showed "Slugg Street" for a long time.

Agnes, at the Mintos' home at School Street, Brisbane, about 1914.

George quickly established a blacksmith's shop on the main coaching and transit route into Brisbane from the nearby City of Ipswich, and places further west and south. It was located in Nash Street, Rosalie village, about one and a half miles from the School Street house. Unfortunately, however, it failed to deliver the anticipated income. Australian farmers tended, by necessity, to be independent and semi-skilled in a variety of disciplines not required by farmers back in Scotland. One example of this was their ability to skilfully shoe their own horses. This was bad new for George, and, learning from previous experience, he decided to diversify. This was almost certainly the reason for him choosing to set up a fruit run, as well as the Smithy.

Of course a fruit run required horses, and one of George's two horses was a well-beloved creature called, by name and by colour, "Ginger". Horses were, at the time, a big part of Queensland life, and there were many of them in the vicinity. There was only one horse that George had a problem with, with the memorable name – "Henry by Metal". His owner, a Mr Batchelor, took great delight in singing his steed's praises

– whose speed and endurance were apparently second to none.

It was only a matter of time until George's competitive nature was stirred, and, confident in Ginger's abilities, he threw down the challenge of a race. A two-mile course was set around the streets of the neighbourhood. By the time the two horsemen urged their mounts across the starting line, the route was lined with excited friends and neighbours. The whole family was present near the finish line, waiting with nervous anticipation to see which horse would round the final bend first. It was with a collective whoop of delight that they welcomed the sight of Ginger, ridden by their father, come thundering across the finish line first.

While George was struggling to come to terms with the new skills required of him in this challenging land, Europe was struggling to cope with a deteriorating political situation. Military build-up had been the obsession of many European nations since the turn of the century. Germany, Austria-Hungary, and Italy had formed a Triple Alliance of mutual defence in the closing years of the nineteenth century. This had been mirrored in 1907 by Britain, France and Russia forming a similar Triple Entente.

By 1914 peace was maintained on a hair-trigger, and as told in Chapter Four, the assassination of Arch-Duke Ferdinand in Sarajevo was sufficient jolt to shatter it.

One by one, over the next few hours, the great powers were drawn into the conflict. Britain became involved as a result of Germany's invasion of Belgium, a country whose neutrality Britain had undertaken to defend, if it were ever attacked. This had been agreed by the Concert of Nations at the Treaty of London, in 1839, which concluded the original recognition of Belgium's independence.

World War I, (known then as The Great War), was fought in a number of theatres, but chief amongst these was what was known as the "Western Front". This was where the full horror of trench warfare was seen. Both sides dug in, along a line comprising four hundred miles of trenches, stretching from the English Channel to the border of Switzerland.

The constant attrition occasioned by use of machine guns, trenches, slow-moving infantry advances, and huge concentrations of artillery fire all caused a stalemate which lasted for years. The British launched their first mass offensive on the Somme in July 1916. There were over a million casualties there, that Autumn, and still the stalemate persisted.

The rest of the world looked on aghast, as so many died in the struggle. Life went on, of course, especially in far away places like Australia. But the shadow of the conflict threw it's darkness into all corners of the earth, and nowhere was immune. One young man in Lugg Street, Brisbane, Australia, had been avidly absorbing news on every major action in the war. He had also been watching the calendar, almost daily. This was Robert Minto, eldest son of George and Agnes.

Robert had been born on 1st August 1898. After he finished school, George made arrangements for Robert to sit the Public Service initial exam and so, by 1916, he had already worked as both a Telegram messenger and then a Telegraphist. He wanted to enlist at seventeen, and initially George refused. Robert proved his endurance by carrying a bag of coal all the miles to the Smithy, after which George signed his papers. However, he was found out and rejected, as being too young. Now he was eagerly awaiting his eighteenth birthday. When this arrived he was thoughtful enough to spend it with his family. It wasn't until the next day that he was going to join up.

He enlisted on 2nd August, 1916, in the 25th Battalion of the Australian Infantry. His father had tried to enlist at the beginning of the War, but had been turned down on grounds of being considered too old for combat. Now, of course, George had the added incentive of wishing to serve alongside his son, and to try to protect him from the worst heroics and follies of youth. But would the army take him this time?

Weeks of worry, and more late night Minto talks followed. In the event, however, the army were pleased to have him, as the Western Front had, by this time become a ravenous and indiscriminate devourer of men.

The ultimate outcome of these deliberations was George's decision, in October 1916, to close the smithy. He enlisted in the 25th Battalion on 31 October, and he and Robert embarked together on H.M. Australian Transport "Desmosthenes" at Sydney on 23rd December 1916, bound for France.

In April 1917, following their arrival in Europe, George sent, as a keepsake, a letter and photograph to each of the four sons that he had left behind.

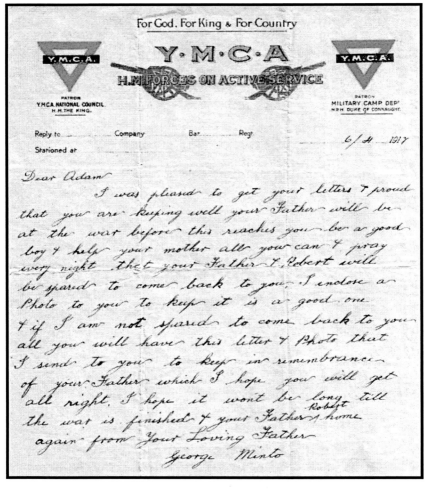

George Minto's letter to Adam, 1917.

George and Robert took part in the April-May 1917 battles of Bullecourt, where the German Hindenburg Line was breached for the first time. That spring saw the loss, (in the same general vicinity), of both of Robert Minto's cousins of the same name. And another casualty of war that summer, (albeit a Naval one) was the faithful "SS Otway" – she who had first taken the Mintos to Australia, back in 1911. She had been converted to serve as a Royal Naval Armed Merchant Cruiser in the 10th Cruiser Squadron. The Otway was torpedoed and sunk by U-boat 49, on the 22nd July, in the Minch, west of Scotland, with the loss of ten lives.

Back on the western front, as summer wore on into autumn, the British began an offensive at Ypres. The Passchendaele offensive, – as it was called – became mired in bad weather, and resulted in some 250,000 casualties on each side. Each of these casualties were lives that suddenly ceased – story ended. In the period 20th to 25th September 1917 the 25th Battalion were engaged in what was to become known as the Battle for the Menin Road. During 20th to 23rd September they undertook an advance towards Bellewarde Ridge, and incurred some casualties, including one officer and nine other ranks. That was the date that neighbours in Brisbane have confirmed that Agnes spent pacing in front of her house all night. She was described as "fey", (second-sighted), and knew the worst already. Some Australian casualties died of their wounds at Polygon wood, east of Ypres, on 23 September 1917, but George survived transfer to the 44th Casualty Clearing Centre. There he "made a good fight to get better and to get back to his wife and bairns". Sadly, his wounds were too severe, and at 11pm the life that had been unfolding since 1873 suddenly ceased, – story ended.

But that's not quite right. No story is ended so long as there is a family that carries on. And in this case there was Agnes, and there were the five boys, although one of them was still in a war zone.

Robert continued fighting on the western front, and was involved in the various battles to counter the spring 1918 German offensive, and those leading up to the German surrender in November 1918. Sometime during this period he transferred from the infantry battalion to the

Division's signals company. He is recorded as returning to Australia on 27 May 1919 after completing his service in "Signals".

Agnes must have been very pleased to see him safely home. The last year and a half had been hard, and, apart from the obvious weight of worry lifted from her soul, Robert's return would lighten her load in other ways too. She had been coping alone with the raising of four sons in an unfamiliar continent, ever since that day in 1917 when she had been waiting for the local Presbyterian minister's visit, and allegedly forestalled him having to deliver his bad news, by saying – "You don't need to tell me. I know George has been killed".

She had also been dealing with the "economics" of the situation. Due to the terrible slaughter of Australians, particularly on the Somme, there were, sadly, many women like Agnes, whose families had suffered the loss of the main earner. The Australian government wasn't unsympathetic to the financial plight of such widows and orphans. It was prepared to offer limited help, such as small hardship loans, in recognition of the sacrifice of the menfolk. Pensions, in today's accepted sense, were still many years in the future, however, and Agnes' Scottish thrift stood her in good stead when it came to the scrimping and saving necessary to support her remaining four dependants.

The situation needed some of that special, gritty Agnes treatment at home too. As the mother of five boys, she fairly quickly began to feel a bit isolated. There was a feeling of relegation to kitchen and domestic chores. She was absolutely not having that. She decided that she was not going to be omitted from family discussions. With her beloved George gone, she felt a duty to be a large part of her sons' lives.

Her sons, and their friends, who played sports like Rugby, Cricket. Soccer, and Tennis would gather in her breakfast room, a large room adjoining the kitchen, from which she would listen to the numerous arguments, some of which, no doubt, became somewhat heated at times. When they were holding their postmortems after the Saturday games she realized she was beginning to simply feel 'left out of it'.

So she acquired books containing the rules of all these sports, and studied them until at least she knew as much as the boys did. From there on she was accepted as an equal. She would have been considered quite a character, in Australia, with her forthright manner and Scottish accent.

Although originally attending the Ithaca Presbyterian Church, Agnes later became a foundation member of the Carmel Presbyterian in Bardon, as it changed from Sunday School to Church. It was within walking distance of her home and was a modest structure, with a single circular stained glass window. It was built of wood, and began life with a slate roof.

Agnes was given a tremendous burden of responsibility having been left with five boys, so far from her natal land. What seems to have carried her through was faith, sheer grit and determination to overcome adversity, and last but by no means least her sense of humour, all of which we shall hear more of in Chapter Nine.

George and Agnes Minto, and their descendants in Australia, are described and listed by Table Five, on page 169 at the conclusion of Chapter Nine.

Chapter Six

American Alarums
and Excursions

*"History can show few benign mergings of people with
people. Flame and blood is always the cement."*
George Mackay Brown

The man stood, almost unmoving, looking out at the street, through the window. He was dressed in his Sunday best. The hat, dark coat, and umbrella completed the picture. As Church Officer he always carried himself with a slightly impenetrable dignity, and now was no different.

Samuel, his son, sat across the room, a blanket placed over his knees. Sam may have been ill, but he was one long way from being stupid. He watched his father with concern. The old man was far more agitated than was at first apparent.

Sam's physical immobility seemed not to dampen his other perceptions. If anything, he noticed even more. Take the way the old man was just running the finger of his right hand almost imperceptibly along the platework and engraving on the front of the umbrella he was gripping. He was tracing and retracing the working of his own name, there in the brass – "D. Allison, Paisley". There was

The Allison Umbrella.

also the frequency with which he had been checking the clock earlier. It was almost time.

David was sixty four years old, and he was now approaching a moment he'd been waiting for, for sixty of those years. The traffic on Underwood Road, outside, merely served to increase his anxiety. John was part of that river of traffic, flowing fast towards him. He would be here in Paisley soon.

As we've heard, David, born in 1846, was the youngest of ten siblings. His elder brother, John, was now seventy-eight years old, and the last occasion when these two respected patriarchs saw each other was shortly after David's fourth birthday. Sixty years! The words seem almost incomprehensible to him. Where did the time go? Will he recognise John? And what might they say to each other?

The questions repeat, in his head, and as he stands there, he begins to remember John's last days with them, so long before. There is always an element of hero worship, when one brother is four, and the other a strapping eighteen-year old, and these two were no different. There was great excitement as the regiment came through Renfrewshire. There were probably good reasons, too, why John had decided to join up, but David was overly-young, really, to grasp any of that. He just remembered the noise, and colours, and hubbub. He remembered his mother's tears too.

When John had gone David felt emptier. There was a place, inside, where the pieces were no longer a perfect fit. He noticed, too, how his mother's embraces, for a short while, were bit more frequent than usual, and she hugged a little tighter than was comfortable. But slowly, things returned to normal. There was, at least, the occasional letter. At first, anyway. But only until 1854. It was the regiment's posting to Bermuda that changed everything. It's difficult to write home with any regularity when you're on the run from the army.

The poor conditions for the troops in Bermuda, and the onset of virulent fevers, left many soldiers dead or dying, and the morale of the rest in tatters.

John felt more than ready to face death on any battlefield required of him. This creeping stinking death that came in the night, bringing cramps, and spasms, sweat and waste, was more than he could take. Watching his friends taken into such a dark and senseless oblivion worked a profound change upon him, and although he knew it was wrong to leave, in the final balance, escape seemed preferable to the end that awaited him, if he stayed.

The last letter that he wrote from Bermuda described the rampant fevers, and was, simultaneously, an explanation for his desertion, and a temporary good-bye to his family. And then he vanished. He did a very good job of that. He never ever made clear, either in that letter, or at any subsequent time, whether his regiment were still in Bermuda, or whether they had relocated to Canada, before he slipped away into the shadows.

Canada was where he ended up though, one way or another. When he entered the United States, he came by way of the Canadian border. There were reasons for this. Given his recent past, it suited his purposes that there was no U.S. immigration record of any arrivals using this route. Not in the 1850's, at any rate.

The U.S. government knew that they had to take action when the numbers slipping into the country by this route reached epidemic proportions. By the 1890's shipping companies were even openly advertising passage through Canada as advantageous for those who wished to avoid U.S. inspectors. It was in 1894, therefore, that the United States put in place the necessary manpower and legislation to process the many thousands who each year poured south across the Canadian border.

For John such documentation was still almost forty years in the future, and so his entry was made quietly, sometime in the four years between 1854 and 1858.

Those four years are a mystery, and are always likely to remain so. Where was he? What was he doing? Was he learning the lay of the continent, and it's burgeoning culture, as he worked his way slowly south, like a migrating bird? That would seem to be the most likely scenario. In any event, it was 1858 that John first appeared in Morrow, Ohio.

This was a small rural village, lying a few miles north-east of Cincinnati, in Warren County. The area was primarily agricultural, and John's upbringing in Erskine was to stand him in good stead. He could use and apply what he'd learned from his father, and so carve a place for himself here, where he could be accepted by his neighbours.

Quiet lives, however, are not immune to disruption by the shadow and consequence of national politics. Hard on the heels of John's arrival in Morrow came the beginning of the collision of American worlds. The deeply felt differences between society in the North, and society in the South were reaching the point where talking was no longer enough. The do-ers were about to do. There were a number of fundamental social and political schisms between Northern and Southern life, but chiefest among these was the issue of slavery.

As early as 1859, John Brown led a raid, by eighteen men, on Harper's Ferry, Virginia. This abolitionist intended to capture an arsenal there, to arm freed slaves in a proposed insurrection. But no slaves rose, and the raiders were quickly captured.They were tried, condemned to death, and hanged by March 1860.

Abraham Lincoln's election as President of the United States, in November 1860 helped to intensify the feeling that politics and economics were moving towards a position where both the Southern institution of slavery and the continuation of the American Union were under threat. Although John didn't fully grasp the enormity of the coming troubles, he could feel the military life rushing upon him again, with the inexorability of a runaway locomotive. The country was now only months away from the savagery of the most tragic conflict in American history.

On 20 December South Carolina seceded from the Union, and was joined by six other southern states to form "The Confederate States of America" in February 1861. In Abraham Lincoln's inauguration speech, on 4th March, he said:

> " . . . *In your hands, my dissatisfied fellow-countrymen, and not in mine, is the momentous issue of civil war. The Government will not assail you. You can have no conflict without being yourselves the aggressors. You have no oath, registered in heaven to destroy the Government, while I have the most solemn one to "preserve, protect and defend" it . . . "*

After fighting began at Fort Sumter, South Carolina, in April, Virginia, Tennessee, North Carolina, and Arkansas joined the southern states in their Confederacy, and so one more step towards all-out war was taken. News of the fall of Fort Sumter inflamed the north, and Lincoln called for 75,000 troops to put down the Confederation. The conflagration was now inevitable.

As the country went up in flames, John Allison was one of the millions caught up in the heat. He enlisted in Company A of the 12th Ohio Volunteer Infantry, a regiment proud to have provided the first company of volunteers "for the suppression of the rebellion" on 13th April 1861. A Union Meeting was being held when news of Sumter's Fall was telegraphed in, so the first company formed right then and there.

This was typical of the first year of the war, when the armies of both sides were little more than huge ill-armed mobs of civilians, attempting to outmanoeuvre each other. Southern generalship was superior, but before long, the north would have the weight of men and equipment on their side.

John served with the 12th Ohio throughout the war. The regiment's first action was at Scary Creek, West Virginia, on 17th July, 1861. The Service record shows that this regiment was in almost continuous action thereafter, until November, when they overwintered in Charleston.

Easter 1862 saw the resumption of hostilities, with much action in Virginia, and the beginning of the Maryland Campaign, as Confederate General Robert E. Lee fought his way brilliantly ever northwards. This advance culminated on 16th and 17th September 1862, at the Battle of Antietam. It was here that Robert E. Lee's northward surge broke, on the dark blue, and resolute, storm walls of the northern troopers. It was here, too, on the 17th, that John Allison was wounded in the head, during what is still described as the bloodiest single day in American military history. John won honours in this battle, and was described by comrades as a brave soldier.

The poignant monument on the Battlefield, which commemorates the 12th Ohio Volunteer infantry has the inscription "This Regiment advanced to this place on the afternoon of September 17, 1862. It moved from extreme left of Union line of battle exposed to a severe flank fire and held their position the remainder of the day. It's loss was 17 men killed and 25 men wounded, total 33". John was one of the wounded, but spent very little time in the hospital. He remained in the forefront of the fighting throughout most of the next two years.

By 1863 the sheer numbers of Union soldiery were shifting the balance of power in favour of the north, and Robert E. Lee's defeat at Gettysburg confirmed that process. The 12th Ohio weren't present at Gettysburg, being engaged in patrol duties on the Ohio River during that period.

By late 1864 the Union had recruited over 2 million men, and the Confederacy had enlistment figures of around 800,000 men. The war continued unabated, with the North's invasion of the lower South. General Grant secured Virginia, which, when combined with General Sherman's victories across Georgia and South Carolina, destroyed the South's armies by the spring of 1865.

Abraham Lincoln was sworn in for a second term on 4th March, 1865, towards the end of the war. His inaugural address was conciliatory:

"let us strive on to finish the work we are in; to bind up the nation's wounds; to care for him who shall have borne the battle, and for his widow, and his orphan – to do all which may achieve and cherish a just, and a lasting peace, among ourselves, and with all nations." . . .

Six weeks later he was dead, assassinated at a Washington theatre by part-time Confederate agent, John Wilkes Booth, who then escaped to the South. None of this delayed the end for the Confederacy, though. Booth, was discovered in a barn in Virginia ten days later, and was shot to death before he could surrender. One by one the Confederate Generals surrendered, through April and early May. By 10th May 1865 the American Civil War was finally over, and those involved had the task of finally moving on from flame and blood, to resume and rebuild their lives. John, who had mustered out in July, 1864, began the job of putting the war behind him, and facing forward, towards a new start, hopefully a bit quieter than his life to date.

Before the year was out, twenty-four year old Mary Farrell was part of the new start that John was enthusiastically building. They were married in Morrow on 2nd November 1865. This domestic life set him to thinking about his own family, and after reinitiating contact, it wasn't long until his younger brother, James (Jim), also travelled to America settling in St. Louis, Missouri.

Letters back to Scotland described how both John and Jim were faring in their new lives. Undoubtedly, tales of Jim's position in St. Louis, and the success of John and Mary's farm in Morrow, influenced some of the next generation to follow in their footsteps.

Back in Glasgow, John's eldest brother, Walter, continued to lead a troubled and often drunken life, and there is almost certainly a link between that unpleasant homelife and the fact that most of his children chose to emigrate. His eldest son, Samuel, eventually went to America with wife Maggie Alexander, sometime after their daughter Elizabeth was born in 1886. They settled in Hoboken, New Jersey.

Samuel's younger brother, named John Allison (like his uncle in Morrow), was a fine-tool maker apprentice. He left this trade, however, and began to put distance between himself and his father, Walter, by joining the 4th Lanarkshire Rifle Volunteers. By 1878 he was a Lance Corporal, and had also become a skilled marksman, winning the Battalion cup for shooting that year.

After leaving the Volunteers, he dallied in Glasgow long enough to attend the wedding of his sister Catherine to Duncan Campbell. Then in 1879, because of widespread unemployment in Scotland, and probably in part due to hearing from his uncles about the opportunities overseas, he too decided to emigrate to the United States. An inscription within a presentation bible places this journey in 1879. His passage was less easy than that of his Uncle Jim.

His voyage was long, and he suffered the misery of persistent sea-sickness. On the final approach to New York one of his shipboard companions, who had pretended friendship, stole not only his money, but also all of his clothes. When he disembarked at Governor's Island, therefore, it was in clothes kindly donated by other passengers, in order that he retain some semblance of dignity when setting foot on the shore of his new home for the first time.

It was fortunate for John, therefore, that his relatives had preceded him, as it gave him a destination to head for, where he could be helped and re-equipped, mainly by his namesake – his uncle John Allison in Morrow, Ohio. He stayed there for a short time, helping out on the farm, until his skills as a fine-tool maker led to an opportunity with the Southern Railroad. He moved to Ludlow, Kentucky, where the railroad's roundhouse and maintenance facilities were located.

While there, he developed a new automatic coupling device, better than that which was previously used. Railroad management were delighted to assimilate this into their operations, but were less keen when it came to recognising or crediting John as the source of the improvement. Slightly jaded, and significantly wiser, he left the railroad and founded a grocery business on Ash Street in Ludlow.

It was about this time that he met Jeannie Buchanan from the neighbouring town of West Covington. She had been born and raised in Glasgow, not far from John's own haunts, and yet they never knew each other until they met as members of the Presbyterian Church in Kentucky. They were married on 13th February 1883, and lived on Butler and Latta Streets in Ludlow, where they had four children over the next five years. The eldest was Sarah Elizabeth (Bessie), born 19th August 1884, followed by Mary, William, (who died in infancy from meningitis), and Jessie.

John had always had an abiding interest in horses, and in the late 1880's this resulted in him purchasing a boarding and livery stable, and becoming an agent of R.E.L. Weaver Undertaking in Pike Street, Covington. His horse-sense, his people skills, and his business acumen all helped to make this venture a success, and when Weaver died in 1895, John became the sole owner.

His popularity and people skills were probably also the reason for his later election as the Sheriff of Kenton County, (in 1914), despite being a Republican in a predominantly Democratic County.

He was still a crack-shot, winning both money and medals, at rifle and revolver competitions across northern Kentucky. His reputation for shooting seemed to earn him the respect of many of his prisoners. When prisoners were unaware of his skill, the deputies made it their business to spread the word. One story illustrates it thus:

"John and one of his deputies are bringing in a particularly rowdy prisoner from a rural area one day. The deputy spots a rabbit, off in the distance, and challenges John to shoot it. John answers – Sure, which eye? – and then proceeds to follow through, with complete success, using his Colt Special 38 calibre revolver. One very quiet and chastened prisoner gives no more trouble. Quite the contrary, in fact. Back at the Jail he decides to be helpful, by explaining to all the other prisoners how the Sheriff could shoot all the buttons off a man's coat, before bringing him down!"

I guess, too, that John would have heard more than his fair share of jokes about the "sharp-shooting Sheriff, who could bury them too".

Before these days as sheriff, and just as the twentieth century was beginning, John and Jeannie made one trip back to Scotland. They were both as seasick as they had been on the original journey outwards, but other than that their visit went smoothly. Whether they visited Walter before his death in 1903 is a matter for conjecture. Either way, when they returned to Kentucky they said that they had accomplished all that they had wished, during the visit.

Some few years after their return, their eldest daughter, Bessie, now twenty four years old, met and fell in love with Charles E. Doerr. He was from Cincinnati, and had graduated from the University there, in 1906 with an M.D. degree. He was completing his internship at the Cincinnati General Hospital when they met.

Immediately the internship was complete, Charles passed a competitive exam to become an army physician. He and Bessie then decided to be married before his first tour of duty, (which was to be Washington D.C.), and so they were married on 30th September 1908, in Ludlow. There is no doubt that this social highlight would have been attended by many of the Allison relatives from Morrow, Ohio. The families had continued to remain close, throughout these decades.

And how had these same decades treated the elder John, back in Morrow? The first twenty years, following his marriage to Mary Farrell, were not free of sorrow.

Mary and John had three sons, but sadly all died, either in infancy or early childhood. Mary, herself, died in 1886, aged only 45 years. Although she, herself, lies in Morrow Cemetery, the three boys were all buried in the Catholic Cemetery outside of town.

Despite these tragedies John remained stoic, and was well thought of, by his neighbours, being seen as hard-working, fair, and popular.

He married again on 1st September, 1890. His second wife was Edie Elvers, born in 1854, and 36 years old at the time of their wedding. Together they worked hard on the land, and even farmers from round about admitted that the Allisons grew the best corn and wheat in the area.

John and Edie had three sons, during the 1890's. John Walter (Walt) was the eldest, born in 1891. Paul Robert (Bob) arrived next, in 1893, and Edwin Ruthwin was the youngest, born on 10th March, 1896.

As his own boys grew, John's thoughts turned, ever more frequently, to those brothers and sisters that he, himself, had left behind in Erskine, half a century before. These were brought even more poignantly to mind while he was listening to the tales that John and Jeannie brought back, after their visit to Scotland at the turn of the century.

Before the twentieth century got any older, and after hearing about the death of his brother Walter, John decided that he wanted to make a last visit back to Scotland, to visit his surviving siblings.

This wasn't, of course, as easy for him as it was for others. He was, to all intents and purposes, still AWOL, (absent without official leave), from the British Army, and that made him, technically at least, a wanted man in Britain. The letters crossed and recrossed the Atlantic, as he and his brother David tried to decide what to do.

Finally, around 1910, David asked his younger son, Alexander, the schoolteacher, to write to the War Office, to see if John could be granted the pardon required to permit him to make this last visit home.

Alexander was happy to give it a try, in the hope of getting the opportunity to meet the uncle he'd never seen. The resulting correspondence was a success, and every day since had brought them closer to this momentous meeting.

It was time. Finally it was time! And now that there were things to do, David's unease left him. He headed out of the door, turned east onto Underwood Road, and walked briskly down to the station. Almost no time later, he was watching the train arrive, in clouds and billows of steam. And as it cleared, suddenly John was there in front of him.

There they stand, a frozen tableau, two elderly men, who have each lived a life different from the other, and between whom there is little common ground. The silence stretches, and deepens, and threatens to swallow them both. What should they do? What should they say?

And then blood calls to blood, and in that particularly understated and austere Scottish way, David nods his head, and says "Aye, John", and John steps forward, hand extended. "Davey, you're looking a bit older", he says, as their hands clasp. The handshake is firm but brief. It is, nonetheless, sixty years deep, and in that moment they both look away, lest the other should see the glisten of a tear in an eye. From that moment too, inside them both, where the pieces had long been out of kilter, everything again felt right at last.

The forthcoming days were filled with words and smiles, the catching up on a lifetime's news, tears, and laughter. The visit was a triumph for everyone involved. And on this occasion, when it was time for John to return to Morrow, it seemed right. He had received a marvellous welcome, and been treated so hospitably, and yet his own growing family in Ohio were calling, and he knew it was time to go.

Four years after his return, the world plunged headlong into the Great War. The background to the war was outlined in Chapter Five. At eighty two years of age this wasn't a war that John was going to have to fight in. Even so, still he felt that military threat rushing down upon him yet again. But this time it was because his sons were the right age!

There was a chance, however, that the Allison boys wouldn't be involved. The first twelve years of the twentieth century had brought record economic growth for America. This, in turn, led to a national indifference in the area of foreign policy, and a lack of concern with events outside of the United States.

When the Old World plunged headlong into the nightmare of the Great War, American President, Woodrow Wilson, asked his citizens to remain neutral in thought as well as in deed.

This position was adopted with the best of intentions, and was tenable until early 1917. It was the German U-Boat threat which metaphorically torpedoed the American position. Over 100 American civilians had lost their lives in the U-boat sinking of the Cunard Liner, Lusitania, in 1915. It was only Germany's promise to suspend submarine warfare that kept America out of the war at that stage. When the Germans resumed their policy of unrestricted submarine warfare in spring of 1917, Wilson felt that he was left with no other choice than to lead America into the conflict.

Bob Allison enlisted in July 1917, and his elder brother, Walt, joined up in May 1918. Their youngest brother, Edwin, who was, by this time, twenty two years old, was already a farmer, and, as such, was precluded from joining up, as farming was classified as one of the reserved occupations.

Walt and Bob were both part of the huge American Expeditionary Force. Of the 4.7 million Americans that had been mobilised, about 4 million of them were in the army, and about half of those made it overseas to the European continent.

Both boys served diligently, during the remainder of the war. Bob, in particular, found himself involved in the greatest American battle of the war – the Meuse-Argonne offensive. The objective was clear – capture the rail node at Sedan, thus disrupting the German rail communication in France and Flanders, in turn causing a German withdrawal from occupied territories.

During October, while Bob's division fought in the Meuse-Argonne, Marshal Foch asked for two American divisions to help the French Sixth Army, and the Belgians, who were attacking to the extreme north. Bob's division answered that call, thus taking part in the Ypres-Lys (Flanders) operation. They methodically overcame the enemy's resistance until relieved on November 4th. Thereafter, they rejoined the Meuse-Argonne offensive and were there when the armistice was signed.

Their cousin, Bessie Doerr, and her husband Charles, had been stationed abroad in the years running up to the war. They had been sent to the Philippine Islands in 1909, and after a number of different postings, ended up at Camp Keithley in Mindinao. It was here that their daughter, Jean, was born, on May 28th, 1910. It was also the part of the Philippines subject to the greatest unrest. The Moros of Mindinao actively resisted the American presence until 1913.

In 1914 the Doerrs returned to the United States, but life got no quieter. One of Charles' postings in 1916 was the Texas/Mexican border, during the Mexican Resistance and the Pancho Villa raids. In 1917 he was posted to Camp Humphrey, a primitive tent city in the Virginia swamps, just south of the nation's capital. The area was drained, and Fort Belvoir was created – a staging area for troops heading for the European theatre of war.

Charles, now a Colonel, designed and oversaw the building of the first permanent hospital at the Fort. It was also during this time that Bessie became pregnant again, and on 8th August 1918, she was delivered of a son, John Charles Doerr.

Eight weeks later the infant, John, was fatherless. The influenza epidemic hit the area with a vengeance, and Charles' new hospital filled up fast, with the ill and dying. Mortality amongst these raw recruits was appallingly high, and the medical staff were driven to exhaustion. This made them yet more vulnerable, and liable to infection. Charles contracted the disease and died 3rd October 1918, aged only thirty five.

The war finally ended a brief thirty-nine days later. An armistice was signed with Germany on 11th November 1918. A significant date. This day is known in Scotland as St. Martin's Day, (Martinmas). It's the day when the spirits of the dead, that have been roaming free since All Souls night, (2nd November), are required to return to the quiet earth. On this particular year one could imagine that, at last, the spirits would gain a measure of peace in their resting.

John Allison's 90th Birthday, 1921.

As the world crept into the 1920's, old John's boys picked up their lives where they had left off. Walt and Bob both worked for the railroad, while Edwin, (the youngest), had already followed his father, and had become a farmer.

1921 was a good year in Morrow, as it was John's 90th birthday. There was a family party, and the cake was very impressive too. In fact it was so impressive that a proud John sent a photograph and note back to his brother David, in Scotland. Many generations have viewed John and his cake since that time.

For now we'll leave the Allisons, at that birthday party. We'll look in on them again in Chapter Ten, and see what the descendants of both "Sheriff" John, and "Old" John have been up to since 1921.

Both "Old" John, and "Sheriff" John, and their descendants in America, are described and listed by Table Six, on page 189 at the conclusion of Chapter Ten.

Chapter Seven

The People and the Places

"For when I dinna clearly see
I always own I dinna ken;
And that's the way wi' wisest men."
Allan Ramsay

These preceding chapters have described ancestral society since prehistoric times. We have gazed into the morning mists until they cleared, to reveal the first Allisons and Mintos, and the places along the valley of the Clyde that were important to them.

For many generations these families continued to live as part of the land, and close to the townships of their forebears. This early history could, if we continue to follow the water theme, be viewed as the sparkling pools of upland water which will later feed our "Rivers Running Far".

By the time of Thomas Minto and James Alason, in the eighteenth century, the peoples of Scotland were, for a variety of reasons, becoming less settled. Time's gravity was being felt, and our "Rivers" were beginning to flow. They ran down through the years into the nineteenth century, and from there out across the world.

North America and Australia were not the only two end destinations. The waters of both families found a confluence here in Scotland too, intermingling in the year of 1921.

This movement of people raises a number of interesting questions. Some of these queries were first mooted, in the prologue (on page 27) and all are central to the emigrant theme. When investigating the process of migration, it's important to realise that "status quo" is a place.

Indeed, it's a place where many people are at their most comfortable. To "take the big step", therefore, is usually the result of changing circumstance. It always requires effort, and is very often painful. The first generation migrant can be heavily beset by feelings of grief and loss, as amply described in the lines of W.E. Aytoun (1813 – 1865):

> *They bore within their breasts the grief*
> *That fame can never heal –*
> *The deep, unutterable woe*
> *Which none save exiles feel.*

There are a suite of questions connected to this, like . . . What causes people to go? Where do they go? What do they experience and how does it change them?

These are questions which we will surely consider, together with associated tales and examples where appropriate, but I don't promise answers. As Allan Ramsay says "when I dinna clearly see, I always own I dinna ken".

Let us start from the premise that, without a reason, no-one would change their essential life circumstances, and that they would continue living in that very familiar place, (known as status quo). Those, therefore, that "take the big step" are motivated to do so by some force, either internal or external. The internal force, or personal desire for change, is usually described as the *Pull*, while the often unwelcome experience of an external force creating unwanted change is called the *Push*.

In reality the situation is just as it sounds. The *Push* involved people being compelled to leave, even though their individual choice would be to stay. The most obvious victims of the *Push* were the criminals, and political/religious undesirables who were transported overseas as prisoners. This latter group, over the years, would have included Covenanters, Jacobites and Radicals. As well as solving the problem of lack of prison space in Britain, it also took these unwanted citizens as far from Scotland's shores as possible.

The most innocent, and heart-breaking, victims of the *Push* were the children who were kidnapped and shipped overseas to be sold as servants in the colonies.

By far the most numerous of the enforced emigrants were those highlanders who had endured betrayal and forcible eviction from their ancestral clanlands.

Economic and social conditions could also be powerfully compelling, resulting in families and individuals having to emigrate, despite their wish to remain in their native country. This was especially the case during the famines and food shortages that afflicted Scotland in the nineteenth century. The collapse of some of Scotland's traditional industries, and the mechanisation of others, led to large numbers of people being forced to seek a better life overseas, to avoid suffering distress, destitution, or even death.

Examples of these economic disasters include:

● The effective end of kelp manufacturing in the 1850's. In kelp-making, seaweed was burned to produce alginate which was used in the manufacture of glass and soap. Following the reduction of the duty on the Algerian plant, barilla, (also used in soap and glass making), the kelp industry collapsed.

● The huge numbers of unemployed handloom weavers who were ultimately offered assisted emigration due to mechanisation within their industry.

● The falling herring prices in the 1880's, which caused distress first in the Highlands, and then later down the east coast of Scotland.

The third of these examples shows clearly the link between economic hardship and emigration, in that the Marquis of Lothian, Secretary of State for Scotland received a petition from the Fisherfolk in Fraserburgh asking for an assisted emigration scheme, which would help them, (some 700 souls), to relocate in British Columbia . . .

"For on no part of the East Coast has the losses arising from the fishing industry fallen so heavily as upon this the central and

most important fishing depot on this coast and the utmost necessity arises that a scheme of Immigration should at once be carried out so that the surplus population may be early relieved from what must end in inevitable disaster".

The *Push* was also felt, even within a social context. Some individuals felt the need to emigrate due to a necessity to evade the law, while others did the same in order to evade undesired matrimony.

More emotive still were those who emigrated because they couldn't face life in Scotland without relatives who had decided to go abroad. Sir John McNeill, chairman of the Board of Supervision for Poor Relief in Scotland, undertook an inquiry in the Highlands, in 1851, five years after the potato famine. One witness, Farquhar Fraser said that although he was seventy six years old he would rather emigrate with his sons, who were unable to find work as carpenters in Scotland, than remain at home without them.

There were a great many other situations and circumstances which resulted in people being forced to move overseas. The last that I will mention here, though, was the general improvement in agriculture in the nineteenth century, which involved many workers, and even small farmers, being displaced from the lowland farms.

The *Pull* factors relating to emigration are a great deal less distressing to examine, dealing, as they do, with hope and desire, and with people's dreams and aspirations.

From earliest times Scotland thrived as a trading nation. Although Scotland's Darien Scheme, (an economic and national disaster) is becoming increasingly well-known today, the country, nonetheless, had many trading successes over the years as well, most especially across Europe, and in what is now recognised as Poland.

This success at the merchant trades led many a young Scot to try their hand at making their fortune, abroad. This fact is of importance because, when allied to the Scots traditions of both the mercenary military profession, and the merchant marine, it shows that Scots over the centuries were well used to the concept of going overseas in order to improve their lot.

As the seventeenth century drew to a close, Britain suffered the convulsions brought about by the end of the Stuart dynasty, and the ensuing Jacobite Risings continued long into the next century. When the Hanoverian cannon smoke cleared, on Drummossie Moor, after the battle of Culloden, the government of the day was left with the question "where the hell do we go from here?"

As we have already heard, one of the answers that was introduced was the recruitment of yet more Scots, and especially Highlanders, into British Army regiments. Allowing Highlanders to wear the kilt, play the pipes, and speak the Gaelic, was a powerful incentive for them to enlist. However, enlistment was made attractive, too, for both Highlanders and Lowlanders, by the offer of grants of land overseas, in return for service.

In the closing years of the eighteenth century Scotland was a land of contrasts. The developments described in chapter three, such as land improvements, mechanisation, and early industrialisation all led to economic improvement for the country as a whole. They did not, however, by default, lead to an improvement in the quality of life for all of the population. In fact, immediate effects included an increase in the numbers of people who were made unemployed, and a rising urbanisation, which led to overcrowded living conditions. Both of these situations were further exacerbated, as we have heard, by the regiments returning home following the Napoleonic wars.

It was to escape conditions like these that people dared to dream of lands of plenty, far overseas. This, then, was the time when people with money chose to emigrate, in the face of displeasure from both the government and from landowners. They were uniformly generally opposed to emigration, at this point in the historical process.

Those people that chose to go overseas were often those with relatives that had already gone before. This, then, was an aspect of a phenomenon noted by James Boswell in his "Journal of a Tour to the Hebrides", written in 1773. The phenomenon that Boswell was describing was the infectious nature of the desire to emigrate.

This evocative passage has been well-used by scholars and writers, over the years, (most notably by James Hunter, in his book of the same name, and also in the lyrics of the rock band – Runrig).

Repeated use, however, hasn't blunted the appropriateness of the passage, and so I, too, will use it here. Boswell noted, while on the island of Skye, how the desire to emigrate was enshrined even in the everyday culture of the locale ; "In the evening the company danced as usual. We performed, with much activity, a dance which, I suppose, the emigration from Skye has occasioned. They call it *America*. Each of the couples, after common involutions and evolutions, successively whirls round in a circle, till all are in motion; and the dance seems intended to show how emigration catches, till a whole neighbourhood is set afloat."

The "epidemical fury of emigration" seen by Johnson and Boswell in the islands, also applied to the Scottish Lowlands, and as we have seen, a number of Allisons followed each other overseas, in just this way, to the United States of America.

The change in the attitude of the government can be charted from around the end of the Napoleonic wars. As unemployment soared, emigration was increasingly seen as a workable solution. This official position was further confirmed in 1846, when the potato famines left so many mouths for the government to feed, and the treasury had insufficient funds for the task.

Assisted emigrations suddenly became a very familiar phrase. Sometimes this financial aid was offered by landowners, and sometimes by the government. As the century drew towards a close, Scottish land shortages were the cause of increasing unrest, and this need for land, in turn, encouraged people to look seriously at the option of travelling elsewhere to seek their fortunes. Travel incentives could relate to a person's profession. This is very likely to be the reason that George Minto described himself as a Farmer – which was not unreasonable, given the range of his skills.

George and Agnes Minto had chosen the path of the emigrant in order to secure a brighter economic future for their children. George was also keen to go someplace where his clever innovations would be used and appreciated, rather than be the cause of difficulties. The desire for this better future was probably the strongest factor influencing their decision to go.

EMIGRANTS' INFORMATION OFFICE, 31, BROADWAY, WESTMINSTER, S.W.

POSTER.

1st October, 1888.

Office Open:—
Every week day but Saturday 10.30 a.m. to 6.30 p.m.
Saturday 10.30 a.m. to 7 p.m. only.

GENERAL INFORMATION
FOR INTENDING
EMIGRANTS
TO
CANADA, THE AUSTRALASIAN AND SOUTH AFRICAN COLONIES.

LENGTH AND COST OF PASSAGE.

The Time ordinarily taken on the voyage, and the lowest rate of unassisted passages to the above Colonies, are as follows:—

	BY STEAMER		BY SAILING VESSEL	
	Average Time.	Lowest Fare. (Liable to change)	Average Time.	Lowest Fare. (Liable to change)
		£ s. d.		£ s. d.
CANADA	9-10 days	4 0 0		
NEW SOUTH WALES	45-52 ,,	14 14 0	About 3 months	13 13 0
VICTORIA	42-49 ,,	14 14 0	Nearly 3 months	13 13 0
SOUTH AUSTRALIA	40-46 ,,	14 14 0	,, 3 months	12 12 0
QUEENSLAND	55 ,,	15 15 0	About 3 months	15 3 0
WESTERN AUSTRALIA	35-40 ,,	16 16 0	3 months	14 14 0
TASMANIA	40-50 ,,	14 14 0	3 months	14 12 0
NEW ZEALAND	45 ,,	16 16 0	3 months	13 13 0
CAPE	20 ,,	15 15 0		
NATAL	26-28 ,,	18 18 0		

PASSAGES.

1. FREE PASSAGES.— CANADA. — To selected unmarried Agricultural Labourers and single Female Domestic Servants (apply to the Agent General). No Free Passages to any other Colony.

2. ASSISTED PASSAGES.— WESTERN AUSTRALIA. — £10 is allowed to Farmers, Agriculturists, and others likely to be useful in country districts; but a deposit of not less than £100 (to be refunded on arrival in the Colony) is as a rule required before any assistance is given.

QUEENSLAND.—Assisted passages are given to unmarried labourers connected with the land, as Ploughmen, Gardeners, &c., and to Female Servants, at the following rates:—Males, 12 to 40, £9; 40 to 55, £12. Females, 12 to 40, £4; and 40 to 55, £12.

No Assisted Passages are given at the present time to CANADA, NEW SOUTH WALES, VICTORIA, SOUTH AUSTRALIA, TASMANIA, NEW ZEALAND, The CAPE or NATAL; but in the case of QUEENSLAND and the CAPE passages at lower rates are given, under special conditions, to Labourers engaged here by employers in these Colonies.

In the case of QUEENSLAND, Land Order Warrants to the value of £20 are given under certain conditions to persons paying their own passage direct to the Colony.

3. NOMINATED PASSAGES.— CANADA, NEW SOUTH WALES, WESTERN AUSTRALIA, and NATAL.—Residents in these Colonies can, under certain specified conditions, nominate their friends for Free Passages on making payments to the Colony as under:—

QUEENSLAND.—Males, 1 to 12 years of age, £2; 12 to 40, £4; 40 to 55, £8; Females, 1 to 12, £1; 12 to 40, £2; 40 to 55, £8. Confined to Agricultural and other Labourers connected with the land, and Female Domestic Servants.

WESTERN AUSTRALIA.—On payment of £7 to a limited number of Nominees, approved by the Crown Agents for the Colonies.

NATAL.—£12 per adult.

No Nominated Passages are at present given to CANADA, NEW SOUTH WALES, VICTORIA, SOUTH AUSTRALIA, TASMANIA, NEW ZEALAND, or THE CAPE.

ARRANGEMENTS ON LANDING.

CANADA.—Depôts for emigrants are provided at the ports of Quebec and Halifax and the other principal towns in the Dominion.

NEW SOUTH WALES.—Apply to Mr. G. F. Wise, Immigration Agent, Hyde Park, Sydney.

QUEENSLAND.—There are Depôts at the principal ports and in various parts of the Colony, in which Government assisted emigrants are received free of charge for a few days after arrival.

WESTERN AUSTRALIA.—There is a Labour Registry Office at Perth where Emigrants should apply, but no Government Depôt for the reception of Emigrants is now open.

NEW ZEALAND.—There are Depôts at most of the principal ports for the reception of emigrants.

There are no Government Depôts in VICTORIA, SOUTH AUSTRALIA, TASMANIA, THE CAPE, or NATAL; but there are private agencies in some of these and the other Colonies, particulars of which are given in the Circulars.

BEST TIME FOR ARRIVING.

CANADA.—April to middle of July—not the Winter months.
NEW SOUTH WALES.—Any month—September to November for preference.
VICTORIA.—Ditto.
SOUTH AUSTRALIA.—May to October.
QUEENSLAND.—April to October inclusive.
WESTERN AUSTRALIA.—September to November.
TASMANIA.—Any month—September to November for preference.
NEW ZEALAND.—September to January inclusive.
CAPE.—Any month—August for preference.
NATAL.—Any month—August for preference.

PRESENT DEMAND FOR LABOUR.

FARMERS WITH CAPITAL.—A demand in all the Colonies.
FARM LABOURERS.—A demand for good men in CANADA, NEW SOUTH WALES, VICTORIA, QUEENSLAND, TASMANIA, and some parts of NEW ZEALAND.
MECHANICS AND GENERAL LABOURERS.—Some demand in MELBOURNE, especially for men connected with the building trades. Little or no demand in any other Colony.
FEMALE DOMESTIC SERVANTS.—A good demand in most districts of Canada and the Australasian Colonies, and a slight one at The Cape.

Particulars as to the state of the Labour Market in the various Colonies from time to time will be given in subsequent editions of this Poster.

NAMES AND ADDRESSES OF COLONIAL REPRESENTATIVES IN ENGLAND.

CANADA.—High Commissioner, 9, Victoria Chambers, Victoria Street, Westminster, S.W.
NEW SOUTH WALES.—Agent General, 5, Westminster Chambers, Victoria Street, S.W.
VICTORIA.—Agent General, 8, Victoria Chambers, Victoria Street, S.W.
SOUTH AUSTRALIA.—Agent General, 8, Victoria Chambers, Victoria Street, S.W.
QUEENSLAND.—Agent General, 1, Westminster Chambers, Victoria Street, S.W.
WESTERN AUSTRALIA.—The Crown Agents for the Colonies, Downing Street, S.W.
NEW ZEALAND.—Agent General, 7, Westminster Chambers, Victoria Street, S.W.
TASMANIA.—Agent General, 5, Westminster Chambers, Victoria Street, S.W.
CAPE.—Agent General, 1, Albert Mansions, Victoria Street, S.W.
NATAL.—Emigration Agent for Natal, 21, Finsbury Circus, E.C.

Further information can be obtained by writing or personally applying to the Chief Clerk at this office, 31, Broadway, Westminster, S.W., from whom the CIRCULARS issued by the Committee of Management respecting the separate Colonies can be obtained gratis, and the new HANDBOOKS, with Maps and fuller information, at the price of 1d. post free for each Colony.

[490] 1000 [M 12]

Printed for Her Majesty's Stationery Office by W. P. Griffith & Sons, Ld., Prujean Square, Old Bailey, London, E.C.

Document 43: AF51/90

Emigration Poster, 1888 – (National Archives of Scotland, AF51/90).

There were a number of other factors, also acting upon them, however, over which they had little or no control. These included the development of the motor-car, the mass-production of domestic ironmongery, and the threatened court action about the patent, for which they had no funds to fight.

It may be fair, ultimately, to consider the Mintos to be a good example of an emigrant family for whom the push and the pull of the process were present in fairly equal measure. They chose Brisbane because of the favourable terms of the assisted passage. They also undoubtedly chose it because they knew something of the climate, the landmass, and the opportunities awaiting them, before they ever took the big step. As emigrants within the twentieth century, they were reasonably well-educated, and would have had foreknowledge of Australia. It was not, therefore, a leap into the dark, but rather, could be seen as a calculated step towards an assured future for all five of his sons. It is also certain that, by travelling as late as 1911, George and Agnes would undeniably have known other Scots who had undertaken the same journey within the previous few years.

For most of us, following any path down which other feet have recently passed is less daunting than striking out into trackless wilderness. This is why we so often find members of the same family, or the same community, following down the same path.

The Allisons' pattern of emigration is a prime example of this behaviour. John Allison, born 1831, seems to have been the first of the family to go to North America, (although even that is by no means certain). John's motivation seems at first to have been mostly the pull that surrounds the excitement of a young man joining the army, and the prospect of adventure for pay. This suddenly darkened, while in Bermuda, into a "leave or die" kind of push-pressure, as some terrible fevers swept the barracks. What fever exactly isn't known, but best guesses include the plague, or cholera.

Once John had deserted from the army, he moved from Canada to Morrow, Ohio. Why Morrow? Was it just coincidence. Morrow wasn't large. Even today it boasts only 1,286 people. One thing we do know about it, however, is that John wasn't the first Allison to reside there.

Were these earlier Allisons second or third cousins, from a prior emigration. that we as yet know nothing of? Perhaps they were, and if so, then John making his way here in 1858 would make perfect sense. The prior century saw many Allison patriots in action at the battle of King's Mountain, South Carolina, in 1780. This was a pivotal battle in the Revolutionary War, and at least six of these Allisons were part of that unstoppable legendary vigilante force – The Overmountain Men, (see Appendix I). I like to think that perhaps these heroes represented earlier Renfrewshire emigrants, and that perhaps one of them, who later settled in Morrow, Ohio, had descendants who became a beacon for John. I hope, one day, to unearth some documentation that will prove or disprove this theory once and for all.

Once John had settled, and began sending letters back to Scotland, it had the effect of creating that well-trodden path, that idea of a safe route through the wilderness. As was so often the case, this led to more members of the family following before long. In our family, of course, this was John's brother James, and then John's nephews, the younger John, and his elder brother Samuel.

Their sister Catherine also emigrated, but to Toronto, in Canada. This in no way dilutes the idea that people follow their own family's trailblazers, however, as this was where her husband, Duncan Campbell, had relatives who had gone out before.

While all of these emigrants were being drawn by the lure of a better life, the three siblings, Samuel, John and Catherine were also trying to escape from the shame and shadow that Walter had cast over their old one.

The idea of the safe route through the undergrowth became reality for James and much later for Samuel, but sadly not for the younger John. For him the wilderness crept in close during his journey, leaving him seriously seasick, and the victim of robbery. The fact that he was on the family "highway" did mean, though, that he recovered himself sufficiently to head along to Morrow, where he could recover, and begin building a new life. Despite his initial difficulties, young John was, thus, able to set up in business, and before long was judged to be a success.

This wasn't a rarity in a country with the opportunities which the United States offered, but neither was it common.

It would repay us, before continuing, to consider the science of "kidology" that was sometimes applied by the emigrant. Put more simply this is the "streets are paved with gold" effect. We all know that this was never the truth, but there were many letters sent back from America to Scotland that conveyed just that idea.

People felt that it was important to give their families the impression that they were doing well, even when that wasn't the case. This wasn't necessarily to do with bragging, Sometimes it had to do with wounded pride, and sometimes a desire to protect those "back home" from worry.

The Seafield Muniments include a letter to John Grant, in Leith, from his son in Baltimore, Maryland. It takes an opposing position, outlining the huge problems that potential emigrants could face, and his view of their likelihood of failure, thus – "their eyes are at last opened so far as to see the folly of abandoning their own homes to seek a precarious subsistence so many thousand Miles across the Atlantic Ocean . . . I can say with great truth…that there is not one of a thousand of these deluded people who, after twelve months experience, do not wish themselves at home again".

These examples – the streets of gold, and alternatively, the thousands wishing to return home – are the extremes, but there is no doubting their effect on people's aspirations, and the choices that people made/make about going or staying.

These questions of push and of pull are nowhere better examined than in Professor T C Smout's classic work in Scottish social history, "A Century of the Scottish People 1830-1950". He spends considerable time considering the relative strengths of each impetus, and sums up as follows:

"the choice of every individual depends on his subjective preferences and on his personal estimate of the advantages of going or staying".

He also made it plain, however, that due to increasing literacy, and increasing availability of newspapers and radio towards the end of the nineteenth century, more people were becoming aware of opportunities elsewhere. The three ambitions most commonly pursued by Lowlanders were the chance of higher earnings, more fun when young, and better prospects of self-advancement. As Professor Smout observes:

"it was obvious that the countryside had little to offer, but the town, or the world overseas, had something. There was a choice, and the Lowland countrymen and countrywomen took it in the belief that they were doing something positive with their lives".

The decision to go was never the whole process, however. As we've seen, these people travelled to other countries, and other continents. They saw strange and marvellous places, and in some cases became part of distant wars. They met many new and different people, and for some emigrants the process was easier than for others. For all of them, though, it was an experience which raises yet more questions.

One of these questions relates strongly to issues of place and culture. To what extent might an Allison born in America differ from his Scottish cousin, and if he does, then how much of that is down to where he was brought up, and how much of it might have been purely character difference, even if they'd been brought up in the same town in Scotland?

These kinds of issues have taxed the great minds of the past, and no satisfactory conclusions have yet been reached. Sometimes, though, consideration of the questions can be as rewarding and almost as illuminating as the gleaning of an answer.

In particular, the topic of "Nature versus nurture" was discussed with enthusiasm by the Greek philosophers, and later became one of Darwin's areas of interest. It's an everyday wording, to describe the contention over the extent to which genetic makeup ("nature") or alternatively life experiences ("nurture") influence a person's character traits or attributes.

Sometimes it's easy to say that one or other factor has been the major influence. Language, for example, is wholly dependant on **nurture**, while hereditary illness, such as Cystic Fibrosis, is **nature** at work. The left-handedness evident in the Clan Kerr is another example of **nature**, while religious predilection takes us back to **nurture**. These, however, are just the simplest examples, and from here on in, things become ever more confusing.

The most common situation is probably one in which there is a mix of both nature and nurture affecting character traits, and people often disagree wildly about the relative importance of each factor.

There are a range of sensitivities associated with the whole nature/nurture question. Few topics are so certainly guaranteed to create major disagreement in those debating the issue. This is due to the fact that when gene–based differences are interpreted as affecting levels of intelligence, motor-learning capabilities, criminality etc., then they can also be used to buttress racism and other forms of bigotry. At their worst, eugenicist policies, defined early, by Sir Francis Galton, have been used as "scientific" justification for genocide.

Frankly, the levels of emotional energy and intellectual fury that are stirred in such arguments seem sometimes pointless, in light of the question of whether the trait being measured is even real, and understood. For example, studies examining the heritability of Intelligence Quotient, (I.Q.), are common, and yet there are still no agreed standards which describe exactly what "intelligence" is.

The biggest unresolved question in this whole area of philosophical study is that of the place of free will. If Free Will makes us who we are, then what place has either genetic determinism or environmental determinism.

The nature/nurture debate provides few hard and fast answers, but is still worthy of consideration here. We can then look at issues of cultural difference, in the knowledge that although these could be described as nurture factors, we are looking at them within the scope of the wider context.

We don't need to dwell too deeply on matters of culture, but it would be remiss to ignore them completely. When we are describing people travelling to the far ends of the known world, cultural questions do have a relevance.

Culture is the learned set of beliefs, values, norms, and material goods that are shared by those of a given group. It can be viewed as the way of life of a people. It shapes their understanding of good and evil, health and sickness, life and death. Most interesting of all, (especially when we are considering the issue of people moving across the face of the earth), it is a dynamic process.

When emigrants come into contact with people from very different cultures they can often experience the feelings of confusion and disorientation known as culture shock. This can result in ethnocentrism, (the tendency to judge the customs of others according to one's own cultural standards), which can lead to cultural conflict. The dynamic nature of culture, however, more often leads to the absorption of new beliefs, and the emergence of a new, combined culture. This is the most likely source of any major difference between Scottish, Canadian, or Australian Mintos.

There may be a humour to the phrase "England and America – two countries divided by a common language". There's a kernel of truth in there too, however, especially when you add both the Australian and the Scots dialects into the mix. Core values, too, are cause for consideration – Are they the same in all these corners of the world? My instinct is to answer "yes", Our values, on all three continents are the old Scots values of freedom, and equality, spiced up with the slightly more modern concept of democracy.

However, it is almost inevitable that there will be instances where there are slight differences in beliefs, values, and norms, between each of these societies. That is probably a very good and healthy thing. Cultural diversity brings greater depths into all our lives. The French probably described it best, with the phrase "Vive la Difference".

So, in regard to the whole topic of nature/nurture, and culture, I say again, and now you see why I say it . . . "when I dinna clearly see, I always own I dinna ken". There are no right answers here. There is only a set of complicated questions. So sometimes the way forward is to just accept that things are the way that they are. At the same time it is possible to rejoice in all the many ways in which we differ, one from another, and the ways in which we enrich each other's lives as we interact. It's also fascinating, despite our differences, and our background, how the faces and characters of our ancestors appear and reappear throughout the generations, no matter how far we travel. Imprints of the past live on longer than we know, and the future is shaped by what has gone before.

Chapter Eight

A Land Fit for Heroes

"To live in hearts we leave behind is not to die."
Thomas Campbell

Stand on the crest of the Gleniffer Braes above Elderslie, in that place between night and day. That tremulous moment just before dawn breaks. Stand there facing west, as time hangs suspended like an indrawn breath, and all is in darkness.

Suddenly, not degree by slow degree, but rather, all at once, come as if unbidden, you can see the shape of the mountains of the west. Then, as the morning lightens at your back, the detail washes into the landscapes before you, like a picture being painted while you watch.

Here you stand, in the land of the ancient Britons, looking west to Argyll of the Scots, which writer/historian Marion Campbell called "the Enduring Heartland". But all directions are equally rewarding. This vantage point affords views north, south, east, and west, over a land steeped in history, and rich in tales. Finn and Ossian from the Celtic Myth Cycles bestrode those distant hills, whilst Elderslie, at the foot of the Brae on which you stand, was the birthplace of that Scottish icon, William Wallace., The struggles of the past have provided more than their fair share of great figures, and this has been a land fit for heroes. But there have been times when this was not so!

The years around the turn of the century were marked by increasing political activism, in Scotland. In the Highlands, discontent over rent increases led to the establishment of a Highland Land League, and finally the setting up of the Crofter's Commission, securing fairer rents, tenure improvements and compensation payments.

We heard how Keir Hardie, inspired by Scotland's Radical and Chartist tradition, worked towards the birth of both the Scottish Labour

Party and the Independent Labour Party. He was also a fervent nationalist, and took every chance to call for Home Rule, in Scotland and Ireland. His socialist principles led him to oppose Britain's involvement in the Great War. It was a time of trouble, and in more ways than those immediately apparent. Many nations of the world were, indeed, locked in armed conflict. But there were underground movements as well.

The socialist doctrines of Marx and Engels had been taking root. Their followers, all the major parties of the Second International, had passed resolutions at successive congresses, most notably at Basle (1913), that the proletariat of the world would never fight in a European capitalist war. When that war came, however, these resolutions were overturned and overlooked in every country except Russia.

In relative terms enlistments were more numerous in Scotland than elsewhere in Britain, munitions production was highest in the Clyde basin, and numbers of war-dead disproportionately higher in Scotland than any other country of the Empire. These are not statistics that paint a picture of questionable loyalty, and yet, as the war dragged on, events in a wider theatre made the government increasingly edgy.

The destabilisation which the war wreaked provided an opportunity for political, philosophical, and economic revolutionaries everywhere. There were anti-colonial revolts across the globe, and also ideological risings. The success of the Bolsheviks in Russia, in March 1917, changed the world, beginning the age of modern revolution.

Scotland had loyally served the Empire throughout the Great War, and unrest on the home front had, in reality, been minimal. There had been some intermittent strike action by Clydeside engineers, and John MacLean had been imprisoned for urging civil disobedience, but other than that, things had been quiet.

The returning troops had been promised "a land fit for heroes", by Lloyd George, the Liberal Prime Minister. As huge numbers of soldiers were demobilized, and returned home, it became apparent that the promised good housing and employment opportunities did not exist. The government failed even to provide civilian clothes for the returning soldiers. "A land fit for heroes" was an empty promise, and unrest grew amidst those same heroes that had fought for King and country.

A shorter working week would have led to more jobs, helping the demobbed troops by reducing unemployment. The Clyde Workers Committee called a strike in January, 1919, in support of reducing the working week to forty hours. This was the incident that triggered the government's paranoia about a possible Bolshevik rising in Scotland. By the following day thousands of troops and several tanks had been rushed into Glasgow to control the population. Riots ensued, and when the furore died down, twelve strike leaders were under arrest, and no rising had taken place.

Russian Bolsheviks had believed that socialist revolution was imminent in the West. It didn't happen that way. By 1921 such revolution was a spent force, and Soviet Russia became more and more isolated. This isolation, although unplanned, was to affect much of world affairs through the years of the twentieth century.

Scotland had its own trials and tribulations, both social and economic, from 1921 onwards. The Wartime production boom had disguised developing weaknesses within the country's industrial infrastructure. Foremost among these was an overdependence on heavy industry, and a requirement to compete with more modern coal and steel production as practised in other countries, (e.g. Germany and the USA).

The capital and skills associated with heavy industry weren't readily transferable to the light industries which more readily developed nearer the large and lucrative markets of the south of England. Thus the sharp downturn in world trade during the 1920's hit Scotland far more severely than the rest of the UK. Unemployment rose sharply, as did the numbers receiving poor relief.

The stock market collapse of 1929, (known as the Wall Street Crash), is well known and documented. This is often cited as the beginning of the worldwide slump known as the "Great Depression", 1929-1939. The causes of this global crisis are still debated today, and we will look at them again in Chapter ten, but perhaps the main point to keep in view here is that Scotland had already been in the grip of economic malaise for almost a decade before the accepted dates for the onset of the Great Depression in much of the rest of the world.

One of Lloyd George's post-war election slogans was "Homes fit for Heroes". He was still uneasy over the George Square riots in Glasgow. The legacy of the radical tradition in Scotland had resulted, at that particular point in time, in the whole country's population being both politically aware and active. His aim was the fairly overt creation of public housing in place of company housing, which would forestall people turning to Bolshevism, and he was heard, at cabinet, to say "Even if it cost a hundred million pounds, what was that compared with the stability of the state". Thus the Addison Act was passed, and although it wasn't wholly a success, it did pave the way for most government intervention thereafter. It also laid the groundwork for John Wheatley's more effective Housing Act of 1924, introduced by Ramsay MacDonald's first-ever Labour Government.

As John Wheatley was a self-taught miner from Lanarkshire, it is likely that he built part of his vision on places like the houses at Waverley Crescent in Lanark. These were among the earliest Council Houses to be built anywhere in Scotland, due to the 1919 Housing Act, (Lloyd George's "Homes for Heroes"). It is no surprise, then, that returning war-hero Alexander Allison, and his new bride, Ruth Minto became the first tenants to live at number 7, which was completed just before they became married in 1921.

The downturn in the economy didn't impact as heavily upon their lives as it did on the lives of those who worked in the heavy industries. Lanark Grammar School continued to provide wages and security of employment. The house at Waverley Crescent was the birthplace of both of their children. Mary was firstborn in 1922, and David followed, two years later, on Hogmanay of 1924. Both sets of grandparents – Allisons and Mintos – were well pleased when these grandchildren arrived. There would be no other grandchildren on either side of the family, due to the loss of Samuel Allison and Janet Allison before the war, and Robert Minto and Mary Minto in 1917 and 1918 respectively.

As "only" grandchildren, Mary and David received many visits from both sets of grandparents, during their early years.

David and Christina Allison, Thomas and Mary Minto,
Rutherford Allison, and Mary Allison.

Christina died in 1925, not long after the get-together shown above, and old David came to live with the Allisons in Lanark. His sale of Woodcliff in Elderslie freed up sufficient funds for the family to move into Balgownie, (a detached, stone-built villa), at 6 Hyndford Road. This house remained in the family until the late 1960's. It was here, too, that the family thrived, despite the difficult world times.

The 1920's were a decade of contradictions. The Roaring Twenties are forever associated with Flappers, dancing the Charleston, open-topped automobiles, and a new liberality. Yet it is also the first decade of the great depression, the time of bread-lines, mass unemployment, malnutrition and despair.

Huge numbers of people began to feel that there was no prospect of betterment in Scotland, and no prospect of any kind of life for their children. However much they might wish it to be otherwise, the future lay elsewhere. This decade, more than any other, was the time "of those who went away". Tom Steel describes the phenomenon perfectly in his book, Scotland's Story:

> *"Between 1921 and 1931, 400,000 Scots emigrated. They left from the industrial Lowlands and from the Highlands and Islands and with her people went much of the nation's skill and self-confidence . . . { } . . . Between 1901 and 1961, 1,388,000 Scots were to leave their native land, equivalent to about two thirds of the natural increase in population over the same period. No country in Europe has ever in history lost such a high proportion of her people."*

The contradictions inherent in the way that the twenties might be described are due mainly to differences in "Means". People without "means" saw few, if any, of the benefits of this period, and all of it's austerity. Families with the "means" to live without hardship did so, and furthermore, were able to take advantage of the improvements in leisure and lifestyle that were being introduced.

For the Allisons, this period is perhaps best summed up in my father's own words:

> *"Our family life, (Father, mother, and two young children), was, as I remember it, very happy and normal. There were family outings; family seaside holidays – Ayr, Millport, and Rothesay; visits to Glasgow theatres – Pantomime, and Desert Song; visiting friends with mother; friends coming to visit; father going*

*on marathon walks with ex-army pals; and, of course, visits from
the Minto grandparents."*

Thomas and Mary Minto visited regularly from North Berwick. This
wouldn't have been at all an easy undertaking by public transport, but,
most unusually for the time, Thomas Minto had a car. Though it's only
conjecture, I like to think that it was Thomas's example that fired his
sister-in-law, Agnes Minto, in Australia., to become one of the first car
owners in Brisbane. Agnes would certainly have seen Thomas and
Mary's automobile on her visits back to Scotland.

The twenties was a time of experimentation. Ernest Hemingway, and
F. Scott Fitzgerald were the literary contemporaries of Jazz musicians
like Duke Ellington and George Gershwin. It was also a time for
invention and technological innovation, especially in America, where
the economy had not been ravaged by the years of World War I. This
was a period which saw the invention of both radio and TV; the shooting
of movies with sound, and in colour; and the development of consumer
goods to complement improvements in utilities and services, such as
plumbing and electricity.

It was an explosive decade, and scientific advancements were not
just confined to industrial technologies, health and medicine were other
areas which advanced greatly during the same time period.

Alexander Fleming, a Scot from Lochfield near Darvel in Ayrshire,
made one of the greatest medical discoveries of the decade. Much
earlier, at the age of fourteen, and following his father's death, he had
been invited to join his elder brother in London, in order to secure a
better future for himself. Much in the way of all emigrants, it wasn't
long until there were four Fleming brothers and one sister, all living
together in the city.

Alexander Fleming studied medicine, and became a Captain in the
Army Medical Corps during World War I, and was mentioned in
dispatches. He was one scientist who became deeply affected by
battlefront experience during the war. He had seen how effective a killer
bacteria could be. More deaths on the front could be attributed to
bacterial infection than to the enemy artillery.

After the war, he devoted his time to finding a chemical that would stop it, and, in September 1928, more by luck than judgement, he found what he was looking for. This was the now-famous mould, which was growing in a discarded Petri dish. The mould which he, thankfully, noticed, before throwing the dish into the cleaning solution. The mould that was killing all of the staph bacteria that surrounded it. So in this way he stumbled upon the great medical discovery of the decade – penicillin.

Fleming presented his findings in 1929, but surprisingly, they raised little interest. He continued the research personally, for a time, but it was a task better suited to a chemist, rather than a bacteriologist. The work was taken on by others, but flagged when some of the researchers left, and others were relocated. The lack of funding for medical research also led to setbacks and problems during these depression years, and it wouldn't be until the 1940's that penicillin became commonplace.

This would save many of the young men who would be wounded during the Second World War, but it would be more than a decade too late for Ruth Allison. The china ashtray which she lifted had only the smallest of rough edges. The tiny whisper of sharply indrawn breath that she gave, as she cut her finger on it, was all out of proportion to the pain, damage and general distress that the tiny invaders in her bloodstream were going to inflict.

By the following day it was obvious that she had a septic forefinger, and she was admitted to hospital as her condition worsened. Amputation soon followed, after which she rallied and improved. Her relapse came as she was almost ready to return home from hospital, with a recurrence of septicaemia, this time racing through her system. On the 22nd of November 1931, this girl, (who had survived being trapped in France at the onset of the war), could fight no longer. Ruth died from a Pulmonary Embolism in Lockhart Hospital in Lanark, leaving behind two motherless children, Alexander as a widower, and her parents, who had now outlived all of their children.

This tragedy brought with it great changes in the lives of all of those it touched, and some of the consequences are of sufficiently universal relevance to the theme of this book that we shall come across them again in Chapter Eleven, when talking of the fragility of threads of knowledge.

In the early years following Ruth's death, Alexander worked very hard to fill the gap. David was only six, (going on seven), and Mary was nine. A live-in housekeeper was engaged, to handle a range of domestic duties. Alexander took the children on long Sunday walks, sometimes even seven or eight miles. During these times he passed on his knowledge of the names and properties of all the flowers, plants and trees that they happened across. He arranged piano lessons for Mary, and dancing classes for both children. But most perceptive of all, he also ensured that contact was, at this time, maintained with the Minto grandparents in North Berwick. My father always said that his school holidays in North Berwick were the best times. Alexander accompanied them in the early years, and organised early morning swimming lessons at the open-air pool. They always looked at the temperature board, groaning at 58 degrees, and cheering if it rose to 61 degrees. My father, with wry hindsight, says that in actuality there probably wasn't much real difference between these extremes.

It was during one of these holidays that David and Mary met their Irish second-cousin, Henry Minto. Thomas' brother, Henry, had died in May 1930, (see chart, page 84), but he left a large family behind, including a son called Henry. This Henry then emigrated to Northern Ireland later that summer, where, on Christmas day of that year, he, in turn, had a son called Henry. This was the Irish relative, visiting his great-uncle Thomas, whom the children met, in the summer of 1935.

Like so many emigrants before him, Henry would later, (in 1955), follow other family members to Canada. There he would follow a career in education, would marry Angeline, and by 1961 he would have two Canadian daughters – Alison, and Adele. Adele's great-grandfather Henry would smile to see the next twist in this tale, which will be most appropriately related in Chapter Eleven.

Meanwhile, back in Lanark, old David had died in 1935. He was 88, but it was a further blow for Alexander, nonetheless. He was now left quite without any family in all the world, except his two children, whom he began withdrawing from as they became robust, and self-sufficient adolescents. He spent more and more time preparing schoolwork, and many evenings from 8pm till 9pm would be spent in the back room at Maisie's, an atmospheric old pub in the Wellgate, reminiscing with ex-army mates.

By this time Mary and David had each developed there own circles of friends anyway, and David and his friends in particular were by this time having daily adventures exploring the Lanark countryside.

Lanark was a town surrounded by dozens of interesting spots, just designed to catch a boy's interest, and to be readily accessible to the adventurous. Choice was often their biggest problem. Should they go to Lanark Loch, or perhaps to the *real* William Wallace cave under Cartland Crags, (the one only *they* knew of), or into the Skinwork Quarry to see it's frogspawn, and other unhygienic contents. Sometimes they went to Donnachie's Farm, where his white horse grazed so temptingly below such a climbable tree. There were a number of bruises sustained in the game of climb and drop, as the wily steed always knew when mischief was afoot, and would wait till the crucial moment before sidestepping.

The summer of 1937 in North Berwick saw a milestone in the young David's life. His father had come for a few days, and, going shopping with David, they returned with a new bike. This greatly enlarged David's orbit, but also ultimately led to less time spent at home, and more areas of friction developing between him and his father. By this time Alexander was becoming more lonely and reclusive, the house wasn't particularly welcoming for visitors, and the children were increasingly looked after by successive housekeepers.

It wasn't just homelife that was taking on a darker tint. The world-at-large was also becoming more tense. Global depression seemed to instil, in some regimes, such fear, (of complete economic and national collapse), that they feverishly worked, instead, to exploit the weaknesses in the world's political and economic situation. This swing to the other extreme resulted in expansionist policies, and was a pattern developing most clearly, and alarmingly, in Japan, Italy, and Germany.

The League of Nations, led mainly by Great Britain and France, had been set up in 1919, and was mandated to prevent any dispute between two countries escalating into general war, as had happened in 1914.

In hindsight, it is now generally accepted by scholars of World War II that the League of Nations might very well have persuaded at least Italy, and possibly even Japan, to abandon their expansionist dreams of empire. Germany, however, under Hitler's regime, proved to be supremely unconcerned by any such approaches. It was a country stubbornly fixed upon world power or defeat. When these three nations, set on conquest, came together, the democratic powers knew that world peace might be temporary at best.

The political manoeuvrings in those ominous days at the end of the 1930's are well-documented in many histories of the time, as is Hitler's invasion of Poland, on 1 September 1939. It wasn't the invasion *itself* that brought Britain into the war, it was Hitler's subsequent refusal, over the following two days, and despite diplomatic pressure, to withdraw his troops. Neville Chamberlain, by 3 September, saw no other recourse but to declare war upon Germany.

When war came, it brought many attendants, such as the black-out; rationing; and Civil Defence. Third Year schoolboys were in great demand as "air raid casualties" to be found and attended to, as practice for zealous first-aiders. David threw himself enthusiastically into both this, and later, Air Training Corps. It being war-time, the ATC was a very much more serious affair than subsequently. It required returning to school in the evening, for navigation classes and aircraft recognition training. The silhouettes learned included those deadly airborne threats – Junkers, Heinkels, and Messerschmitt, – and there were also day-trips to airfields.

By 1940 all was not going well with the war in Europe. The June evacuation of British Troops from Continental Europe, through the port of Dunkirk, is now legend. What is less well known is that, following Dunkirk, there was a real and ever-present fear of a German invasion of Britain. As a direct counter to this threat, many senior boys, from school 4th, 5th, and 6th years, were required to take the next school term out, to work in forestry camps. In David's case it was a forestry camp at Innerleithen. This was near Peebles, and involved cycling there at the start of the term, and returning the 38 miles home the same way, at the end of term. The boys were cutting trees, ready for others to set them up as poles in fields, to stop expected glider landings. The glider landings never materialised, and the whole term proved to be an enjoyable interlude.

The boys were billeted in the loft above the stables at the big house, and were required to sleep on palliasses, (straw-filled mattresses). David found that the straw tended to rope into the most uncomfortable knots, and so at the earliest opportunity he went up to the hills behind the house, to cut heather as substitute mattress filler. It was so springy and comfortable, ("like a feather bed!"), that it was no time until all the other lads were following his example.

By the time David returned home from forestry camp, Mary had gone to begin a year's domestic study in Edinburgh. This was then followed by three and a half years nursing training at Glasgow Royal Infirmary in order to attain State Registered Nurse status. Just two years later and it was David's turn to leave home. He had long had an ambition to become a doctor. Now, his choices were complicated by his desire to join the RAF. His father thankfully set up quite a clever double-bluff, suggesting that he start in medicine, initially studying up to the second professional exam, after which he go to the RAF, returning to finish his studies later. David agreed that this was a reasonable compromise, and headed for the Royal Infirmary in Glasgow. Thus, his first year overlapped with his sister's final year.

Mary's next posting was two years at the Sanatorium in Lochmaben, in Dumfries and Galloway, in order to gain experience and certification in dealing with infectious diseases such as the dread killer, tuberculosis.

Tuberculosis is known to have been one of mankind's greatest scourges, from earliest times. The Mummies of ancient Egypt carry evidence of TB, even though they are more than 5000 years old. As a single causal factor, it is responsible for the largest number of deaths in history. One estimate suggests that it has destroyed one billion people in the last two centuries. Known as "consumption", an appropriate name for this destructive process in the lungs, the real tragedy of this disease was that it frequently affected young adults in the prime of their lives. Before streptomycin was discovered in 1945, the treatment involved a lot of fresh air – with beds being taken outdoors – a lot of rest, and a good diet. The diet was supplemented by raw eggs and raw meat, (to give an easily digestible form of protein and fat into the diet).

At that time the Lochmaben Sanatorium had 142 beds for extreme cases of TB and an adjacent 30-bed hospital for infectious fevers. Dumfries and Galloway did not get streptomycin until 1950, but after that there was a rapid decline of TB in the region.

Finally the war drew to a close. Germany and Italy had both surrendered by May, and Japan by September, 1945. It was an uneasy time, with a world learning, hesitantly, how to deal with peace. David continued studying medicine in Glasgow, and Mary had another year to complete at the Sanatorium.

In 1946 Mary undertook the year training, in Midwifery, in Robroyston, Glasgow. She followed this with three years service in the Willian Smellie Maternity Hospital in Lanark. Then, as the 1950's were beckoning, (and having achieved the three entry Requirements – State Registration, Midwifery, and District Nursing), she embarked upon the Glasgow University Health visitor course which would provide her with her professional career from that time onwards.

It was also in 1946 that David met Margaret Macdonald, and thus set the events outlined within the prologue in motion. As with any tale, the flow of narrative carries us through the years, sometimes quickly, sometimes slowly, and most usually forwards. It brings us, at last, to that day in September 1967, when Alexander died, aged 84 years, and his name was inscribed beside that of his beloved Ruth, on a memorial stone in Lanark cemetery.

Ultimately, if you follow this narrative to it's logical conclusions you will find not only me, (busily typing this tale in the hope that it might bring you some enjoyment and enlightenment), you will also find my siblings, their children and mine, and all of their descendants, down all the rivers of time and place. These are the rivers that run the farthest. Their tales belong to the future, and I will make no prophecies here, leaving the recording of their stories to be undertaken by some storyteller yet to come. For now, I will take us back, to visit with those who went away – the various Mintos and Allisons scattered across our world, and to see how the passing years have treated them since 1921.

Table Four, which follows, details the descendants of Thomas Minto, and David Allison.

A Land Fit for Heroes

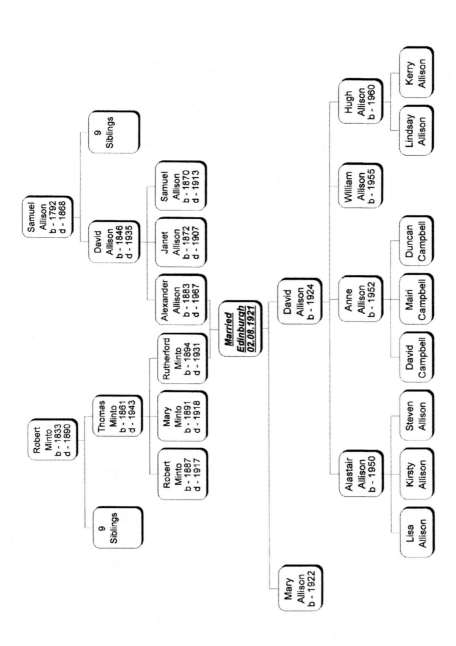

Union and descendants of Mintos and Allisons – from Robert Minto and Samuel Allison, the marriage of their grandchildren, Rutherford Minto and Alexander Alliso in 1921, and their descendants thereafter.

Chapter Nine

The Children of
the Otway

"Seek the beginnings, learn from whence you came,
And know the various earth of which you are made."
Edwin Muir

Dusk had arrived, and on this continent the light went faster than I was used to. Furthermore, to add to my problems, the first batch was not a success! The cooking surface wasn't level. As this was a family picnic, in the midst of a public park, I was attempting to cook my mix on a barbecue with a cooking plate which sloped downwards to a hole in the midst of the hot surface. It was through this hole that my oatmeal mixture kept enthusiastically running.

Perseverance is a virtue however, and help and advice was forthcoming from many sources. Once I had been relocated to a barbecue within one of the park shelters, both better lit, and better suited to my product, (i.e. – no central drain in the hotplate), there was no stopping me. Within a few minutes I think we might have been making history. I was serving what I suspect to be the first ever batch of Highland Oatmeal Breakfast Pancakes to have been cooked in bulk on an Australian Park Barbecue, al fresco, to serve in excess of thirty people. (See recipe at Appendix II).

It was the 7th March 2004, and I had landed at Brisbane Airport three days previously, early in the morning. Judith Minto had met me, identifiable as promised, by her straw hat. The Airport was air conditioned, but immediately we stepped through the automatic doors and into the waiting world I could feel the difference. Even though it was only about 7am the heat was building.

This was my first visit to Australia, and I peered avidly from the car as it wove through the Brisbane suburbs. Judith played "guide" with aplomb. *There* was the Brisbane River, where the Otway came in. *Here* was a good example of an old-style Queenslander house. *This* was the area where George and Agnes first stayed.

Finally, we pulled in to our destination, – Reg and Judith Minto's house, where I would stay for the next couple of nights. Reg met us at the garage, as the car was put away, and seemed so genuinely delighted to be meeting a relative from Scotland that he appeared to be lit from within, with a gentle light of welcome. As he and Judith invited me inside, I knew then that this odyssey of my own, to "the farthest reaches of the world", was going to be alright, – enjoyable and fulfilling in family terms, as well as worthwhile and productive as a research trip.

Reg is the oldest of the Australian Mintos now. George and Agnes' five sons have all gone, the last being Tom, in 2001, aged 94. But the new generations remember, and within these families are held photographs and documents, but most especially the stories and anecdotes that honour the lives of those who came before. Reg is the oldest grandchild, as son of George's eldest boy Robert. Reg's memories and boxes provided my initial data, but the material and the stories that I was given by all family members combined to draw the detail of the earlier generation as follows . . .

By the end of the War, and Robert's safe return, George was 18, Henry 15, Adam 13, and Thomas 11. All of the boys had attended Ithaca Creek Primary School. On leaving school Adam sought, and received, his mother's blessing on a change of name to Alan. He felt that it was a more common name, attracting less in the way of jibes.

Tom won a scholarship to Brisbane Grammar, becoming the first of the family in Australia to have had a secondary education. In addition to academic achievement and being the dux, he also captained the Brisbane Grammar School Rugby Team.

It was in 1922 that Tom, the youngest, left home. Agnes had read in the newspaper that the Federal Government, (at that time led by Billy

Hughes), was offering apprenticeships in the Federally owned Government Line of steamers. There was a place for one boy from each State, providing that they were the son of a deceased soldier. Tom applied, was called to interview, and offered the place. Boarding the tram for home that day, he saw his mother sitting on a seat not far away, and looking at him inquiringly. He nodded, and was then amazed to see his mother burst into tears. Tom himself said "such an outward display of emotion by a Scot was unheard of". That was when he realised that he was leaving his home and family, and only the thought of his older brothers passing judgement stopped him from shedding tears too.

The 22nd November 1922 was the date that Tom went to sea, signed for four years on the Jervis Bay, a passenger and cargo vessel on the England to Australia trade. It also marked the day when all of Agnes' boys were now out in the world, working. Yet no matter how far they travelled, and how their lives diverged, they remained close, and continued to support both their mother, and each other, through the years. These same four years, 1922 to 1926, saw much else happening too.

Robert "Digger".

George "Pod".

Robert, (known as "Digger" as he'd been in the trenches), had returned to a guaranteed job with the Postmaster General's Department. He married Beatrice Kiorgaard, and moved into a house on Coopers Camp Road in Brisbane. Their firstborn, and Agnes' first grandchild, Reginald, was born there, November 1925.

George had become a Fitter and Turner, working in mining engineering. In 1924 he went over to Scotland, and enjoyed the

Henry "Harry".

Alan "Sleuth".

Tom "Little Tim".

chance to get re-acquainted with his Scottish relatives, such as both his Uncle Henry, and his Uncle Thomas. He spent about three months living and working on the Plenderleith farm at Sornfallow and, all in all, had a wonderful time.

Henry was by now a Cabinet Maker and unparalleled craftsman. Due to his genius in creating concealed dovetails, he would later join the team making the presentation suite for Prince Edward's visit to Australia. However, Henry was also starting to show his true colours as an intense but troubled individual, who would, from time to time, be in bother of one sort or another.

Alan was serving a seven-year apprenticeship in the leather trade just as synthetics were coming into use. This represented a serious threat to the future of Saddlery, as many household goods were made of leather, from suitcases to collar and stud boxes.

Before leaving the Jervis Bay, Tom lifted the brass doorstep into the apprentice quarters, and in the space beneath placed a list with all the Apprentices' names and dates of Service.

There were occasions, during the 1920's, when all the boys made it home to Lugg Street at the same time. This was always cause for celebration, but also for brotherly disagreements and arguments. One such difference of opinion centred on the cross- bred fox terrier, Prince. The question quite simply was "which brother did the dog love most?" They decided to all walk in different directions, to see who the dog would follow. Henry tried to rig the outcome, by carrying meat in his pocket. Alan, however, discovered this, and was ever after called "Sleuth" by the others.

There is no doubt that Agnes required a great deal of patience, through the years. She also had concern for the future of her sons, as the twenties slid towards the thirties, and the great depression. She coped with her worries and responsibilities through an outspoken mix of good humour and strong moral standards, all expressed without fear regardless of rank or privilege.

This woman, whom Reg knew as "Grandma Minto of Paddington" worked hard, fund-raising for hospitals and churches, and giving practical gifts to those in greater need than herself. She passed her love for Scotland on to her grandchildren, and even went back to visit with her Scottish relatives, on a couple of occasions. One of her most frequent, but good-humoured, phrases was "Och! You colonials" This was usually said at such times as when her grandchildren were attempting butter AND jam on their bread, rather than one or the other.

Robert Burns wrote his poem "To a Louse" upon seeing such a creature upon the hat of a grand lady sat before him in church. There is an interesting Agnes Minto story very similar in theme. She was sitting in a church pew behind an elderly lady made up in powder and rouge. Agnes took note that despite the outward display of sartorial elegance the lady apparently rarely washed behind her ears. Agnes, from then on, (but only in the privacy of home), referred to the lady as "Auld durrty ears".

Reg helped me to build a picture of how this family of Scots ruggedly created a life for themselves, in a faraway land. He spoke with feeling and affection for all his uncles, and in particular he remembered his Uncle George's ability as a storyteller. "Not the least of his skills was as a raconteur. One never tired of his stories. I can still see him sitting in the corner, more often than not in Henry's rocking chair . . . going on and on with his adventures . . . I can still recite many of these stories." Some of those stories that Reg could recite are now gracing these pages, together with some of his other remembrances. Most striking of all was his vivid childhood memory of the big cabin trunk at his Grandmother's house, with the printing "RMS Otway" on the lid.

I moved on, the night before the picnic, to stay with Alan Minto and family. Alan is the son of George and Agnes' son Alan. Here too, hospitality flowed, and I felt very at home, in their house in Strathpine, (an interestingly Scottish sounding suburb).

I met with many other members of the family the next day, at the Ashgrove picnic, and all of them welcomed me with an enthusiasm which I found heart-warming. Everyone had a huge amount of catch-up to do with everyone else, and the day passed in a welter of children's laughter, background chatter, smiles, and, as the light began fading, the ubiquitous eating and drinking.

Next day I was to head north for almost a week, with Joan, a daughter of George and Agnes' son Alan. I was to be taken to Monto, a place I had seen pictures of and dreamed of seeing for over 20 years.

The Mintos are well scattered across Australia now, and the reasons for that are probably twofold. Firstly, (as Geoffrey Blainey explains in his work "Black Kettle and Full Moon"), Australians are a notoriously mobile people, and secondly, the Great Depression caused the brothers to cast a wide net, and be prepared to travel, in order to find work. Geoffrey Blainey explained it thus:

"The typical young man longed to be on the move. Whereas Americans in the last fifty years have been moving easily from state to state, Australians in 1900 were probably more migratory. The succession of gold rushes spurred them to pack bags and swags and to travel. The shearers were nomadic. Even the first generation of farmers was footloose.....The high proportion of unmarried males in the population also made for mobility, facilitating the folding of tents and moving on."

Visiting Monto was, for me, the realisation of a long held dream. Of course I never met Alan, as he had died in 1996 . But I was well hosted by both his daughter, Joan, and his grand-daughter Jane. I also, most surprisingly, got the opportunity to see and hear Alan, as he had been the subject of an oral-history video-recording before his death. So here, too, I learnt much more, first-hand.

Alan completed the leather-working apprenticeship after seven long years, only to find redundancy awaiting him on the day he became a journeyman. He never worked at his trade. The depression deepened, and he was unemployed for eighteen months. During this time he stayed with Agnes in Brisbane. Finally, his brother, George, who was working up north, got in touch, to tell him that there was work in Gayndah. He lost no time in getting there and getting stuck in. The job in question was smashing concrete, day-long, with hammers. It was back-breaking, and the workers' fists cracked and bled, until some resorted to urinating on their hands to make them better-seasoned for the hammers. At least it was a job, and Alan kept at it, until a better opportunity arose. He became an engineer, arriving in the Monto area in the early thirties. He helped to set up the Monto Butter Factory, and settled in town thereafter. It was shortly after this period that his brother, George, married Nell Muir, and all three of his children were born in the thirties.

Henry continued to live nearer the edge than his siblings. He had charm, and a way of piquing a lady's interest. But there was a danger and a wildness to Henry that sometimes went too far. He was described as being "a law unto himself", and was a staunch believer in trade unionism. He thought apprentices should be paid more, and often found himself out of work, when he would resign from jobs as a sign of solidarity with sacked apprentices. He was still recognised as a master craftsman, but was sometimes a liability too.

It was probably due to this attitude that Henry found himself unemployed in the early thirties. George was at this time a mining engineer at the Gold Mines in Kalgoorlie, and again, as with Alan, he offered to help. Henry headed out there, and George settled him in as a Diamond Driller, with George's mates carrying him for a couple of weeks, until he learned the ropes. Years later he worked for Peacocks, helping create the display at the National Industrial Association Show. What they didn't expect was that he would turn up at the show drunk that year, and insist on going to sleep on his display bed.

The Depression years were years of excitement for Tom Minto. He was still at sea, had served on a number of ships, and taken part in a number of adventures through this time. The secondary school education which he had received stood him in good stead, and he wrote marvellous articles about these years, many of which have since been published in "Australian Sea Heritage". During the depths of the depression he was 3rd Mate on the Junee which went to the Southern Ocean on a fruitless search for the Danish sail training ship the Kobenhavn. He later wrote a book about that quest, "The Search for the Kobenhavn"

Tom qualified for his Master's ticket in 1933, and a year later he paid for his own fare to Scotland to watch over the construction of a new Australian ship, the Manoora.He was to sail with her as 4th Mate when she completed her trials. It was during this visit that Thomas met his Scottish bride-to-be, Cecilia Walker. They were married four years later, in 1938. Similarly, Alan married his sweetheart, Phyllis Collins, the following year in Brisbane, and his brother Robert was his best man.

Robert and Beatrice were living quietly, and Robert was slowly but steadily climbing the Public Service promotional ladder. Reg had been joined in 1930, by a younger brother, called George, (like his uncle and his Grandfather).

This was the George I was to stay with on my return from Monto. George has his Uncle Henry's cabinet-making tools, and he also has an excellent memory full of the many humorous anecdotes concerning family members. Finally, after a last night with Reg and Judith I was back on a plane and heading even farther south.

This time my destination was Sydney. I was met at the airport by Jim Minto, oldest son of Tom Minto. Jim took me to his daughter Elizabeth's home, where, with others, I had dinner with Elizabeth's father-in-law, Robert Fraser Dodd. Good company and chat about Scottish-Australian ties passed the hours away. And then, when Robert told me that his ancestor was transported for treason, a most interesting story unfolded.

I promised, in Chapter Three, that we would hear more about how the legacy of those who were transported overseas after the Radical War lives on. Amazingly, although I wrote that chapter before travelling to Australia, here now, in front of me stood the direct descendant of the youngest of those insurgents to be transported from Scotland following the Bonnymuir uprising on 5th April 1820.

Robert was also kind enough to gift to me a publication called "The

Scottish Radicals" authored by Margaret and Alastair Macfarlane in 1975. It is a work described as making a serious contribution to the serious study of Australian history.

Dr. Hazel King, (formerly Senior Lecturer in History at the University of Sydney), states in the foreword that "The Scottish Radicals were not a typical group of convicts for, unlike the great majority of those transported, they were political prisoners . . . nor were they a typical group because all but one of these Scottish convicts were skilled artisans, and literate. Therefore, some of them left letters and other written sources of which the authors have been able to make good use."

Robert's ancestor, Alexander Johnston, was just a youngster of fifteen at the time of the uprising. However Captain Peddie of the Yeomanry was impressed by his bravery, describing him in a later letter thus "A lad, Alexander Johnston, escaped into the morass and fired his pistol as fast as ever he could load; when the brave and generous officer, Hodgson, perceived it, he shouted to his troops – Save the life of that spirited boy!" Youth or not, he was still sentenced, with the rest, to fourteen years transportation.

The publication concludes that "It is not certain how many of the Scottish radicals returned to their native land. However, from available evidence, it is thought that most of them remained in the country to which they had been banished and where they had made a new life for themselves and their families . . . Their descendants have taken their place in the professions, in politics, in the business field, on the land and in all walks of life, having inherited the industrious, resolute and enterprising characteristics of their Scottish radical ancestors"

And of course, here was Robert Fraser Dodd, standing right in front of me, a living legacy of the Scottish radical war, and one whose characteristics were now flowing through the veins of some of George and Agnes' descendants.

The next day Jim drove me to his house in Woy Woy, north of Sydney. As you walk in, it is immediately noticeable that Jim has inherited his father's love for the written word. There are books lining the walls. Here is a house full of research potential for me. And so, in between Bush walks, and trips to sites of Aboriginal Art, Jim and I begin to sift through the boxes.

Jim was actually born in Bondi in May 1939, just before World War II began. As Tom thought he might be away on long voyages to Britain during the war, he suggested that Celia and Jim go to stay with his mother in Brisbane. They did, for a while. But it turned out that most of his voyages were to Indian Ocean ports, so they returned to Sydney, and moved into a house in Bronte, in 1941. Agnes was, of course, a frequent visitor.

Celia and Tom were always close. There was one night during the Sydney blackout that Celia became very agitated. Tom was away abroad, voyaging afar on the surface of the world's seas, but due home sometime soon. Celia became more and more restless, till Agnes asked her what was wrong. "He's out there, I know he's out there, those ships lights must be his!" she cried. "Don't be so daft" was Agnes' practical reply. But nothing would deter Celia from flashing the verandah lights 3 or 4 times,– sending out into the black vastness of the Pacific. There was a moment's pause, then Tom's delighted answering light came winking back through the dark, as his ship slid northwards through the night, not far off the New South Wales coast.

It could be said that Tom's war began a couple of years earlier, in 1939, when he was appointed First Mate of the Manunda, a Defence-Equipped Merchant Ship. She was requisitioned in 1940 to be fitted out as a hospital ship.

The Manunda left Australia in October for the Middle East on the first of 4 trips. In January 1942 she sailed for Darwin, where the next five weeks were to be spent. Tom notes that from 21st January onwards a rigid blackout was enforced not only onboard the Manunda, but also the American Naval units, and the various merchant ships that arrived. It was only the Australian Navy that continued to be brightly lit, night after night.

Thomas Minto's report, known as "The Minto Report", and titled "Some truths about Darwin and the Air Raid of the 19th February 1942" highlights some further points. Tom describes how the only oil and water lines run along under the main wharf. As he points out, and as many other naval officers pointed out to their superiors, months before the raid, "it is a simple matter to float oil and water lines out to a buoy, fitted with a control valve; or they can be laid along the bottom of the sea, safe from enemy action, and brought up to a buoy with control valve. These are not theoretical but actual methods used in many ports of the world – but not in Darwin."

Tom also heard of a furious argument between the skipper of the troop transport ship Mauna Loa and shore authorities. The Mauna Loa had recently evacuated hundreds of troops from Port Moresby in New Guinea, and they were now on the open decks of the ship. The Naval officers ashore at first refused the skipper permission to unload these troops. The skipper said " Well, I'll run the ship aground up in the mangroves and land the troops that way. We will be bombed for sure and those men won't stand a chance out on the deck." The skipper got his way and hundreds of lives were saved. Had the ship not been unloaded, the troops would have gone to the bottom with the Mauna Loa the next morning.

There were forty-five ships in the harbour, and two thousand people ashore, when the Japanese swept down upon Darwin. The leader of the raid, Mitsuo Fuchida, who had distinguished himself at Pearl Harbour, found this to be an irresistible target. One hundred and eighty eight planes heavy with bombs attacked Darwin out of an almost clear blue sky. They flattened civilian areas onshore, and targeted many of the ships in the harbour. The metaphor about shooting fish in a barrel was close to the truth of the situation. In the midst of this offensive, some Japanese planes also seemed to deliberately attack the hospital ship, Manunda, regardless of it's non-combatant status. More bombs were dropped on Darwin during the course of the raid than had been dropped at Pearl Harbour, and the element of surprise was a factor common to both attacks.

Thomas Minto was on duty as all of these events unfolded, and described them in his own words. This is recorded as the Minto Report, part of which later ended up in the Australian War Museum in Canberra:

"At 1005 hrs. on the morning of Thursday 19th February, out of a lovely sky with a few clouds, we got our first taste of enemy action in Australian waters.

No matter what has been written elsewhere, the first warning the shipping received was when the first bomb hit the wharf. Then the sirens went ashore. The depot ship Platypus was a bad second.

The wharf was burning near its inner end, Barossa and Neptuna at the wharf both appeared to have been hit and the Neptuna was on fire. Zealandia, about 500 yards away, was on fire. British Motorist was sinking by the head. U.S.A.T Meiga was on fire aft and sinking. Mauna Loa was down by the stern with her back broken. Tulagi was nowhere in sight. Port Mar was in trouble. The remaining merchant ship seemed to be O.K. We were undamaged.

On the Naval side, a Catalina Flying boat was ablaze on the water. An American destroyer, ablaze aft, went dashing across our bows, missing us by inches, and steering with his engines. Another American destroyer was on our port side, a solid mass of flame with burning oil around him and what was left of the crew jumping into the burning oil. We manned our motor lifeboat with four of a crew and went to their rescue. They eventually picked up over thirty badly burnt and wounded men; other boats later picked up a few more.

I could hear the planes again, and took time to look up. I saw the Japanese coming over in perfect close V formation, at what seemed to me about 8 to 10 thousand feet and no more. They ignored the anti-aircraft fire and I saw a perfect example of pattern bombing. I saw the bombs released and followed their flight. They straddled the Neptuna at the wharf.

There was a pause and then a ball of orange flame about 200 feet high or higher, and a shower of debris. The Neptuna was blown up and one half was lying in front of the wharf on its side; the other was about five feet above the water. It drifted down with the tide a little and then sank.

Then it was the Zealandia's turn again. Once more perfect bombing, and she was on fire from stem to stern, eventually sinking within the hour.

On the other side the British Motorist was not sinking quickly enough, so the formation gave her another stick and she turned on her side and sank.

Meanwhile we were getting other boats away to pick up survivors when the dive bombers arrived. I did not see them as I had all my attention on the lifeboat, but I heard the roar of his engine and his machine guns blazing. Then there was a terrific roar, and the Manunda rolled from the effects of a near miss, which we later discovered.

This killed four on board and put 76 holes and over a hundred deep scores in our plating overside, and played hell with our gear and upper works. We got our wind back and carried on when we heard the same thing again. There was a terrific roar and debris flying around everywhere. The bomb had missed the bridge and pierced the music room skylight, exploded at 'B' and 'C' Decks, doing terrific damage and causing many casualties. The hit and near miss between them killed nine of the crew and three military personnel, including one nurse, seriously injured seven and caused about forty minor injuries. The after end of the ship still functioned as a hospital unit. Our own boats and naval launches brought the wounded alongside, so that by nightfall we had seventy six patients on board.

The onshore administration in Darwin fell apart as the first bombs dropped, and to this day Australians joke darkly that "one fella didn't stop running till he got to Melbourne".

The Manunda was hit several times, suffered heavy damage, and was evacuated to Fremantle laden with casualties. Tom was less than pleased with what he heard when they arrived – "After eight days we got to Fremantle where we heard Prime Minister Curtin's announcement that Darwin had been bombed and 35 people were injured during the two raids. Funny thing, that. After all, we had 260 wounded just on board the Manunda itself" The Prime Minister is also quoted as having said "the results of the raid were not such as to give any satisfaction to the enemy." Tom always reckoned that, in that case, the enemy must have been very hard to please.

Tom was subsequently awarded the MBE for his efforts during the bombing. One shipmate later described him thus:

"Tom was down on the decks amid the turmoil, overseeing first aid to the ship's superstructure that had been smashed by bomb blast and to the hull that had been holed like a colander. But his concern was not only on board – he had his men lower lifeboats into the harbour cauldron to pick up burning screaming bodies . . . and I still see him in the motorboat leading our little flotilla on this amazing errand of help for the victims of this horrific catastrophe. Tom was truly amazing. He was magnificent."

The MBE was dated 2nd July 1943, which was the same year that he was appointed Captain of the Aldinga.

Meantime, just one month after the Darwin raid, in March 1942, the Japanese were over-running South-East Asia. Tom's elder brother, George Minto, was at that time working at a tin mine in up-country Burma. The Japanese planes arrived without warning, and in strafing a train full of passengers in the station, killed both the driver and the fireman.

George and his mates first became aware of the situation when someone burst into the bar where they were enjoying an off-duty rum. "Can anyone here drive a train?" was the plea. Being an engineer, George was confident that driving a train wouldn't be beyond him, ("after all", he said, "it's just a big engine"). So he and his friends commandeered the train, and with axes cut wood for the fire along the track, getting water out of creeks as they travelled. They ran before the Japanese offensive all the way, and were the last train into Rangoon, saving the lives of all the passengers aboard.

At Rangoon they boarded a British cargo ship and crossed the Bay of Bengal, sitting on deck. When the Captain found out George was a fitter and turner, he persuaded him to stay on the Mollers Line ships and serve with the Merchant Navy through World War II. Some of that service was in the Mediterranean, sometimes near Tobruk.

It was while working as chief engineer on the Leon Chow that

George had his next narrow escape. The Commodore of a convoy, in which George was sailing, ran his ships too close inshore near Alexandria. The Leon Chow ran aground, and had to be left behind. Rumours of enemy ships and planes in the area added a sense of urgency, as the crew struggled to think of ways of refloating her.

George came up with the only workable idea. He waited until half an inch before high water, under the keel. Then he screwed out all the safety valves in the engine room. At this point no-one could have walked past the fire-box door without being sucked into the inferno. The plan worked, and they even managed to catch the convoy before it reached Gibralter.

Once the ship was unloaded in Britain, the Skipper insisted on shutting down the engines. Once they were off, those engines never went again. Still, the crew had been saved, and it's worth mentioning that although the ship was 27 years old, to ensure escape, George had managed to coax 2.5 knots more speed out of her than she had achieved during her original trials.

Henry also fought during World War II. He enrolled 1st July 1941 at Paddington and was discharged 28 December 1944. He was a Private in the 62nd Australian Infantry Battalion, and served mainly in New Guinea. His war record was more chequered than that of his brothers. There was no problem with either his courage or his initiative. He was well able to show these strengths while his battalion was repulsing the Japanese landings at Milne Bay, New Guinea. This was also Australia's first victory against the Japanese in open battle. No, the problem lay in him still being a "law unto himself", and therefore periodically falling foul of the army's authoritarians. It was also not unusual for him to be in receipt of fines or sanctions for drunkenness, and going AWOL from time to time.

His style of rakishness still attracted the women, and it wasn't unheard of for he and a partner to win dancing competitions for being able to waltz flawlessly on the head of a beer keg.

It was around this time, however, that he had a big romance, which for once, actually meant a bit to him. It subsequently failed, after which he seemed to drive himself ever closer to the point of no return, in terms of hard living and carousing.

Neither of the remaining two brothers saw active service in World War II. Alan was deemed unfit on the grounds of his deafness. He had been the victim of an explosion at Mt. Larcombe in 1939. A tin of phynol blew up, and the resultant blast caused him severe burns, hospitalisation, and progressively worsening deafness. He was proud to help the war effort, however, in his reserved occupation at the Butter Factory, where his engineering expertise kept things going despite the parts shortages.

His daughter Joan felt that Alan would have shown far more of his gentle, but marvellously dry sense of humour had he not been compromised by his loss of hearing. She tells many stories by way of example, and one of these was the description of a family outing, in which she was driving south in her usual hurry. Alan was in the back seat, and when Joan came quickly round a corner on a steep downhill she found a huge lorry moving slowly downhill in front of them. She applied the brakes, together with a prayer or two, and they screeched to a stop. The luggage hurtled forwards from the trunk, and fell all round Alan. Without pause he looked over the disorder, smiled broadly, and said "Good driving skills, what was it you wanted from the luggage".

Robert was Traffic Officer in charge of the main metropolitan telephone exchange in Brisbane, during the war. He didn't see active service due to his age, and reserved occupation. Being a veteran of the First War, it follows that by the time Henry joined up, Robert would already have been advancing fast on his middle forties. In fact, time was passing so quickly that by 1943 Robert's eldest boy was actually old enough to enlist for WWII. This was Reg, and he did enlist, in the Royal Australian Air Force. He trained as a medic, in Victoria. Although he never fired a shot on the front line, he did have some hard and formative experiences, such as dealing with the aftermath of horrible accidents involving mid-air collisions during operational training.

Finally, in 1945, the war was over. That year, and the next, saw the boys, this time including Reg, returning home to resume their lives.

Robert decided to transfer to the newly formed Commonwealth Immigration Department, and ended his career as Director of Immigration, North Queensland. Reg told me that his dad reckoned that being Scots was a great advantage for someone working in immigration. "The Scots are great at mixing with everybody, and very good at integrating", he would say, and their house was often busy with Serbs or Albanians or whoever Robert had brought home that day for a meal.

During the course of the war George's eldest child, Jean, had died, aged 8. The emotional fallout from this, coupled with the strains that the war imposed, led to George and Nell becoming estranged for many years. It's satisfying to know that eventually they got beyond all the hurt and recrimination, and did eventually reunite. Their twilight years were spent happily together, which gave their children, Don and Denise, a chance to learn more about the Minto heritage, and the various earth of which they were made.

At the end of the war, however, George, finding himself to be on his own at that time, returned, along with Henry, to live with Agnes in Lugg Street.

Some four and a half years later Agnes, now 73 years old, fell seriously ill. Burning with fever, she was rushed to hospital. Despite investigations, the medical staff couldn't identify what was wrong. When the time came she just turned her face to the wall, exhausted. The death certificate stated that, on 12th June 1949, she had died of "Pyrexia of unknown origin".

After Agnes' death, George and Henry continued to live together in the Lugg Street house. They lived and played fairly hard, and Henry, in particular, worked in a variety of different jobs over the years.

There was a morning, about six years after Agnes died, when Henry complained that he couldn't go to work. Worried, George asked if he needed anything. Henry reassured him that it he was just feeling a bit crook, and if George would just leave him a bottle of water he would be fine. George left the water, but far from being fine, when George returned from work, Henry was dead. Complications related to the heavy alcohol consumption had finally blown out his bright but troubled flame.

Reg, as the oldest of the following generation, was still in his twenties when Henry died, and Alan as the youngest, had just turned three. The passing decades have rung the changes. A further two generations have made an appearance since then, and all four of Henry's brothers lived to see grandchildren. Tom even managed to get to know some of his great grandchildren.

We have heard so much about these brothers that it would be remiss not to fully record the dates of their passing, here below:

Robert Minto – 1979
George Alison Walker Minto – 1977
Henry Minto – 1955
Adam Walker Minto (Alan) – 1996
Thomas Minto – 2001

There was not one of the five of them that was unaware of their beginnings, from whence they came, and the various earth of which they were made. They all described themselves as being Scottish, right to the end. And yet, in the spirit of integration, they were equally proud that their children were Australians.

Regretfully, I missed my chance of meeting any of the brothers. I was, however, lucky enough to meet many of their descendants and their spouses, and that was a genuine privilege. All of these are the people whom I met, while out in Australia. There are currently around seventy of them, of which about half got to the Ashgrove picnic.

I could reach into their lives too, and splash them across these pages. But I don't think that the tale would wish to be told in that fashion. The lives of those that make up the present generations will be suitable material to be moulded into a book once we have all stepped onwards elsewhere. Perhaps the daughter of Tom's great grandson Hamish, or the son of Alan's great grand-daughter Lara may choose to write the tales of all of our lives. And perhaps that would best be attempted sometime around 2065. That sounds like about the right timescale to me.

The Children of the Otway

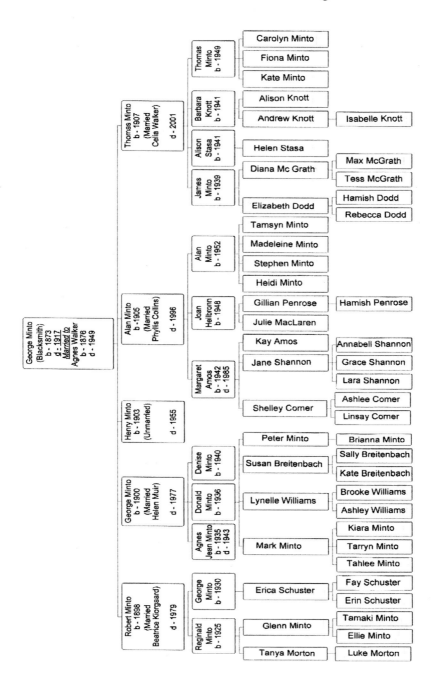

Mintos in Australia – the Australian descendants of George and Agnes Minto (1873 to the present).

Chapter Ten

American Patchwork

"Liberty was ever the tradition of my fathers,
and, among us, no person avails, but rather reason."
Saint Columbanus

The field of Antietam lay, sombre and crusted with ice, under a grey gun-metal sky. A biting March wind circled aimlessly, and muttered, low, amidst the snow and broken ground. I stood, for some time, by the monument to the 12th Ohio Volunteer Infantry, and let my thoughts course free across the unquiet slopes.

The Civil War was a convulsion which undid belief in the new democracy. All the hope that the fledgling Americans had invested in this new land became tarnished.

Loss of innocence, as is so often the case, came with baggage, and that baggage shaped the nation's psyche thereafter.

One result of the conflict was that America became a colossus in hiding. Already leery of being drawn into the politics of the old world, the United States now found wounds and schisms all their own, which needed time and privacy to heal. This ultimately resulted in the adoption of isolationist policies. These same policies, (when bolstered by internal economic success and growth within the domestic market in the early twentieth century), led to America's reluctance to enter the First World War.

Eventually, as we've heard, circumstances led President Woodrow Wilson into the war. When hostilities drew to a close, in 1918, he was determined to sit at the table with the Allies, and negotiate the just peace that was necessary to create the conditions that would usher in a world safe for democracy.

Laudable though this aim was, it was not to be. Europe was overcome by the same corrosive hatreds which America had learned to master following it's own civil war. For now, the Allies' attention was largely taken up with demands for retribution, and by feuds and bad blood that refused denial. America withdrew, done for the moment, with the effort to reform Europe.

A scant two years later, in 1921, Old John Allison celebrated his 90th birthday. How often had he thought of Antietam field, and the civil war, six decades before? And did he ever give thought to me, or someone like me, treading the field more than a further eight decades later. Possibly not. But it's hard to be sure. Especially in places like these, where records are written in bold, the paper is thin, and the pages between times turn restlessly. As I walked the ground almost 150 years later, and charted the action on this tragic field, I felt closer to John than at any time in my earlier research.

It was March 2005 and this was my first sortie, out and about, since the plane had touched down at Washington Dulles International the previous evening. My hope was that the next few weeks here in the USA, visiting and talking with the descendants of both Old John, and Sheriff John, would furnish me with a fuller picture of both of these men. I hoped, too, to capture a greater sense of the unfolding events of the twentieth century, as I walked the walk, and met the Allison descendants now scattered across America.

I met many people on this journey, and I gathered many emigrant tales to bring home, consider, and recount.

As I travelled, I gave frequent thought to that birthday party, held in Morrow, in 1921, (see page 118). The twenties brought mixed prosperity and the USA was in better shape than many other countries around the world. Greatest stability, however, was found in the industrial and financial sectors. At this time the Covington area in Kentucky was economically reasonably buoyant, and the younger John Allison was achieving continuing success as a Funeral Director, with offices, laboratory, and stables on Pike Street, (described as being the largest such business in Covington).

John and Jeannie had three daughters. Mary, the middle girl, never married. Bessie, the eldest, had lost her husband, Charles Doerr, in the 1918 flu epidemic. Jessie's husband, Brice Fleming-Fields was killed in a train accident in 1922. John therefore had all three daughters to care for, and that fact is often cited as his reason for choosing to purchase the roomy and handsome Victorian Mansion at 58 Kenner Street in Ludlow, Kentucky. This house is sometimes still described by local historians as the "Allison House", and was purchased around 1919.

The Allison House, 58 Kenner Street, Ludlow, Kentucky.

It was in 1925 that John entered into partnership with Porter Rose, and so the "Allison and Rose" alliance began, – a partnership name that has endured in Northern Kentucky until the present day. He was active on a number of fronts throughout the community. These included membership in the Ludlow Presbyterian Church, the Knights of Pythias, the Odd Fellows, and the Board of the local fire insurance company. He was also a Director of the Citizens National Bank – which was one of the very few that would survive the storm which was about to hit all such institutions in 1929.

John retired in 1926, at least in name, from the undertaking business. However, he continued to be involved in the larger decisions throughout the first few years of the Great Depression. Although he lost a significant portion of his personal savings in these years, the firm prospered. In fact, John was able to watch with some satisfaction as Allison and Rose relocated, in 1932, to the fine premises that they still occupy to this day. This historic building, which I was later to visit, was the Madison Avenue home of a Dr Tebbs Ranshaw.

John and Jeannie's fiftieth wedding anniversary was the following year. It was on that day, the 13th February 1933, that John lost his beloved Jeannie. It was a scant two months later that he, inconsolable, followed her into death. His grandson, John Charles Doerr, always said he died of a double broken heart – the first being due to his wife's death, while the second was diabetic cardio-myopathy. He left his three daughters, and his grand-daughter and grand-son occupying the "Allison" house in Ludlow.

The family of the elder John Allison, in Morrow, found the Twenties to be a greater challenge than did their town-dwelling relatives. In agriculture, and in the raw materials sector, increased production throughout the twenties led to declining prices. This was exacerbated by wages lagging behind profits, which in turn created a drag on the development of domestic markets. Rural areas in America became early victims of the imbalance between agriculture and industry, and also harbingers of the collapse that was yet to come.

As in rural counties anywhere, in times of vulnerability, people sought a variety of income streams. All of John's boys had at least two jobs. Edwin, for example, worked at the Peters Cartridge Company, as well as farming. Bob was principally a railroad employee, but also bought a farm, in Mason, to supplement the family income.

Old John still lived on the Morrow-Rossburg Road with Edie until August 1928, when, at the end of a long and full life, he died, aged 97 years, on Friday, August 3rd. His younger brother, David, back in

Scotland, would survive him by a further seven years.

I heard these stories, and more, from the descendants that I stayed with, and my first meeting was with John Allison Doerr, (son of the John Charles that was born in 1918). John is Assistant Dean of the College of Agriculture, at the University of Maryland. He currently lives in Ellicott City, a town that, with some justification, describes itself as "A European style city in the middle of Maryland". Ellicott City, indeed, has considerable charm. The attractive stone buildings seem to spread haphazardly uphill from the Patapsco River, and are interestingly punctuated by a mix of historic spires and towers. Main Street, however, provides the unifying thread needed, climbing gently from the river, past the firehouse museum, and through the commercial heart of this small mill town.

My greatest surprise, however, was when John drove me out past the Patuxent Female Institution, and I got my first view of the eighteenth century mills, and mill housing, along the wooded river valley. It was with breathless astonishment that I took in this panorama, so like New Lanark, where my own father walked and played as a child. The two towns are almost just different views of the same place.

Ellicott's Mills were established in 1772 by the three Quaker Ellicott brothers, from Bucks County, Pennsylvania. They chose the banks of the Patapsco River as they apparently saw the area as being "uniquely" suited for providing water power for a mill. Not so uniquely, as it transpired, given that David Dale found an almost carbon copy location, an ocean away, at New Lanark, on the River Clyde, only a couple of decades later, in 1795.

There are, nonetheless, some stories which relate only to Ellicott City – it was, for example, the site of America's first railroad terminal, which was built in 1831, and it was here, too, that the legendary race between Peter Cooper's steam engine, The Tom Thumb, and a horse drawn vehicle, took place.

John, and his wife Joan live above the historic district, where the country opens out into rolling tableland. My time with them was enjoyable, and, as well as good food and good company, I was also treated to some good ideas and information, in the field of family research.

Joan is a Leslie, and is intensely interested in genealogy. She is undertaking some research into her parents family history, in Iosco County, Michigan, and has brokered a fantastic arrangement with the local Genealogical Society in the Iosco area. I include the broad outline here, with Joan's agreement, in the hope that similar schemes could perhaps be begun by others reading this. The Society sends Joan copies of the Tawas Herald, 1896-1928, at no charge, and she can use them to research family history. In return, as she is an accomplished typist, she types an index with name; date; issue; page; and column number, and she emails this back to them, for use in their website, and they now have over a million names on their database.

Joan introduced me to another initiative, of which I had never been previously aware, called Random Acts of Genealogical Kindness. This is a great gathering of interested volunteers, willing to undertake genealogical research (expenses only) in return for the favour being reciprocated, for themselves, and/or others. This involves thousands of people, willing to do many things, from photographing gravestones, through to researching Probate, wills, etc. Unsurprisingly, the website is entitled **www.raogk.com** and I hope that in mentioning it here I may be helping to increase it's volunteer base, even by only a little.

Eventually it came time to leave Maryland, and so I bade farewell to John, and Joan, and boarded a plane bound for Cincinnati/Northern Kentucky Airport. There I was met by my third cousin, Greg Allison. He is Bob's grandson, which makes him Old John's great-grandson. And he *was* great. He asked what I wanted to do that afternoon, and he didn't even flinch when I replied with what had to be the oddest programme he'd ever heard – "I'd like to go to a graveyard, followed by a funeral home, and finish up with a visit to the Jail!".

This first day in the Cincinnati area was spent mainly in Northern Kentucky, tracking down people and places that related to Sheriff John. As Greg is descended from Old John, and not the Sheriff, this stuff was as new for him as it was for me. First stop was Highland Cemetery, Fort Mitchell. Snow blanketed the ground and fell thickly from the sky. There are over 40,000 burial sites in Highland, and so it was a relief to find the office open. Soon after, armed with a map, and clear instructions, we headed deeper into the grounds, and deeper into the worsening snowstorm. It was only brief moments later that I was standing, beneath the trees, and in front of the Allison Memorial, looking at Sheriff John's final resting place. The moment was perhaps more melancholy, and more powerful, than I expected, due to a landscape muffled in snow, and a world muted by a thousand downward spiralling flakes.

It was still snowing, half an hour later, as we stood outside the Allison and Rose funeral home. I went inside, and spent some time being shown around. The whole establishment still exudes a lushness, and a sense of the opulence of yesteryear. I was pleased to see John Allison's portrait, still occupying a place of prominence on the wall, and better even than that, the current owners generously gifted me a book entitled "The Allison and Rose Funeral Home – A History". This volume obviously has special significance as a family keepsake, but has also proved invaluable as a research tool.

Our last stop that day was the Sheriff's Office, in Kenton County. Sheriff Chuck Korzenborn had invited me to visit, while in the area. It transpires that Sheriff John Allison was a particular inspiration to Sheriff Korzenborn, who had already taken time to study much of Sheriff John's life. It was an interesting experience, visiting the court-room, and Sheriff's Office. I gifted Sheriff Korzenborn with all the material I had thus far written, regarding John Allison's life, and for his part, he swore me in, as an Honorary Deputy Sheriff of Kenton County, Kentucky. This wasn't something I had foreseen happening, and yet it was a moving experience, as it put me right inside John's life and times.

John had amassed a vast collection of confiscated guns of every shape and size from all the rogues that passed through his jail. After his death in 1933, his daughter Bessie, who detested guns, allegedly disposed of his whole barrel of guns by tipping them into the cistern at the Ludlow Street House, where they may still be to this day!

Bessie was as well known in Northern Kentucky as was her father. She played the part of civic leader only too well. Local parades often included Bessie Doerr, waving from an open-topped car, and amateur 8mm film has, more than once, captured her, officiating at a local event.

As we've heard, when the Great Depression hit, in 1929, it was widespread. The slump in agriculture worsened, industrial production faltered, and unemployment became endemic. For the whole of the 1930's fully a quarter of the total labour force lacked jobs. Times of crisis, by their very nature, bring out the best and worst in different people. In Bessie it brought out a driving desire to help as many folks as she could. She became a tireless crusader, placing unemployed people in jobs of one sort or another. Every time she heard that someone's home, or future, was in jeopardy, due to unemployment, the news would set her running. She would travel round all her acquaintances, until she was sure she had secured a job for the individual in question. A job in the Ida Thomas candy business here, a job on the railroad there. She also showed, by example, the talents necessary to survive these difficult times – caution and practicality, mixed with community-mindedness. Many of the people that she helped remained firm family friends who continued to visit her through the rest of her life. Her grandson, John Allison Doerr, in Maryland, has gone so far as to tell me that he actually met many of these people, but until his adulthood, had just thought that he had abnormally large numbers of uncles and aunts. It was only afterwards that he appreciated who they all were, and how his grandmother had fought the Great Depression head-on, and won most of her battles.

My grandfather received a letter from Bessie, in July 1940. This time her intention was to deliver relatives from the dangers of the Second World War. Put simply, her letter offered sanctuary to the children of her cousin, back in Scotland:

"The papers tell us that many children are being sent to this country for the duration of the war. Would you care to send the children over to us? I would be glad to do what we can for them, if that would please you. Allison, (my daughter), says she can help to make them comfortable, if they should come".

The children in question, however, were, by this time fifteen and eighteen years old, so my grandfather elected not to send them. In hindsight, I'm quite grateful for that, because my father might never have met my mother, had he been sent to America in his teens, and consequently I wouldn't be around, at all, to be sworn in, as a Kenton County Deputy.

With our business in Kentucky finished for that day, Greg drove me across the Ohio River, through Cincinnati, and onwards to Morrow. Rather in keeping with the "dear departed" theme for the day, Greg's mother, Carolyn, took us to Morrow Cemetery, to see the family plots. There Old John Allison rests, lying between his first and second wives, Mary Farrell and Edie Elvers. After the cemetery we drove to Greg's house, where, as well as his sons and his rumbustious dog, (Beckham), I met his wife Angie. She's the computer user in the house, so it was lovely to meet the person with whom I had been communicating this past year.

Later that night it was time to meet yet more of the living. I spent a wonderful evening at the Valley Vineyards Winery with nearly a dozen of Greg's close family relatives. It was with surprise and delight that I learned that as well as a Carpenter, Greg was an enthusiastic homebrewer of beer. In fact, it transpires that my visit had already been the cause of some debate and questioning by others in Greg's beerdrinking fraternity – (including brother Lonny, and brother-in-law, Lance). "Does he drink beer?"exclaimed one, "He's from Scotland, isn't he? If he doesn't drink beer he must be an imposter!". I'm happy to say that I proved not to be that imposter, and was so impressed with Greg's homebrew that I took some home with me.

I also visited the Warren County Museum in Lebanon, and the Salem Township Public Library in Morrow. It was in the archive drawers of the latter establishment that I found a little gem known as the "Morrow Song", and I have included it for everyone's enjoyment and frustration, at Appendix III.

After the Library, Greg and I managed to track down the Old John Allison House on the Morrow-Rossburg Road, using a mixture of old maps, and an upfront cheerful door-knocking technique. This is the very same house that Old John was photographed outside, on his 90th birthday. On that occasion, (see page 118), he was sitting outside the wash-house and summer kitchen, nearer the rear of the building.

John and Edie Allison's House, Morrow-Rossburg Road.

Old John had twelve grandchildren. Only two never made it into adulthood. They were both of the boys who bore his name – John Allison!

Walt's youngest child, John, died at the age of two. The cause of death recorded was toxaemia, (allegedly from the lead in the paint on the porch railings, which he had a habit of chewing on a regular basis).

Edwin's youngest child was also called John, (known to everyone as Johnnie), and the tale of his passing has become almost family legend. It's an affecting story, and even now, as we discussed it, there was more than one moist eye in the company.

Johnnie was just fifteen, and was widely known in the Morrow area. A sophomore at Morrow High School, he was popular and well-liked by everyone. Since his earliest years he had helped in many ways on his parents farm, and was also involved in good works at the school through the years. Now it was June 1944, and his friend Sandlin Gillen was back on a furlough from the armed forces. Sandlin, Johnnie, and others, had gone to pick up Sandlin's mother. Once she was aboard there was no longer room for Johnnie inside the car, and so he rode the running board.

Appearing as if from nowhere, an oncoming car crowded them off the road, and Johnnie was pinned between a tree and their vehicle, as they swerved from the edge of the road. The culprit failed to stop, and the shocked occupants of Sandlin's car were left to do what they could for Johnnie. Despite their efforts, Johnnie died upon admittance to Blair Brothers Hospital in Lebanon.

He was buried three days later in Morrow Cemetery. Sheriff Hufford never managed to identify the driver of the other car, and Johnnie's surviving family, over time, rebuilt their lives. But they never forgot him.

One of the best aspects of my visit to America has been the enthusiastic sharing of knowledge. I have been gifted a bag-full of priceless information, but at the same time I have been able to return the favour by providing a wealth of other data which might otherwise have been lost. One of the most affecting documents amongst the collection I took to America is the obituary for young Johnnie. I was glad I had taken it, as a number of my relatives had never seen it. When I read it I thought "If anybody writes anything even one tenth as good as that for me when I go then I'll be doing well". It is probably the finest obituary I

Johnnie Allison, at a young age.

have ever read, and so I include it at Appendix IV. One of the last expeditions I went on, before leaving Ohio, was with Kathy, (third cousin of mine, and grand-daughter of Edwin). She took me to see Young Johnnie's grave, and even more raw, she took me to see River Road at Fosters, where he was killed. This was all the more poignant for Kathy, because Johnnie was her uncle.

The next morning I was on my travels again. This time I was flying down to Wilmington, North Carolina, where I leapt into my hire car, (ready for four days of adventurous driving across state), only to find the steering wheel gone. Once I got out of the passenger side, and sat in the driving seat, everything went much more smoothly.

This is really the "heartland" of the emigrant Scot in the USA. This is Cape Fear River Country, where large numbers of Highlanders, Lowlanders, and Scots-Irish all settled. I believe that on North Carolina Tartan Day in 1997, Governor James Hunt said that 'North Carolina has the largest number of people of Scottish heritage of any other state or country in the world'. This included Scotland, and was a genuine claim. My first sortie out, at the wheel of my Pontiac Grand Am, was to cross the Cape Fear River, and head north for the National Battlefield at Moore's Creek Bridge. That was a good decision, as I ended up having a long and useful talk with battlefield staff, Tim Boyd and Linda Brown. This in turn gave me greater understanding of the political issues for emigrant Scots at the time of the battle, (see pages 52 and 53).

Then I headed out, through South Carolina, and up to Columbus, in the mountains of North Carolina. This was the place where I was to meet the one and only American relative that I had actually met before. He had come to visit us in Scotland when I was about fifteen years old. That earlier visit doubtless sowed some of the seeds resulting in my interest in far-flung family. But this forthcoming meeting was still a bit daunting. His name had come up repeatedly, during this visit. The varied and distant American branches of the family might not know each other, but it seemed that they all knew him, (or knew of him). So I thought of him as the American patriarch, or perhaps as the mortar that was holding their stonework together. I needn't have been worried about my stay. As soon as I arrived I was made to feel welcome and at my ease. I was pleased to be there, and within minutes I knew that I was going to enjoy this visit with John Charles Doerr, and Sylvia, his wife.

On entering his study, there was a moments pause, while he decided which of the filing cabinets full of family data was the appropriate one for my visit. There is a veritable treasure house of information here. One batch of cabinets carries the Doerr information, back to and before the time when the grandparents of his father, Charles Doerr, immigrated. They had been hoteliers, and vinegrowers, back in Germany. Another group of cabinets was devoted to his Allison heritage, through his mother, and his Scottish grandfather, the Sheriff.

The final repository of family knowledge relates to the family of his wife, Sylvia. She was born in the Czechoslovakian town of Brusperk, in Moravia. It was a very old community, which developed in the fifteenth century, probably around the year 1420. The house in which Sylvia was born had one heavy roof-beam which carried the date 1747. It was also a fairly stable community, with good records, and little social upheaval. This was a blessing which was to stand the people in good stead, after March 1939. That was when Hitler forced Czechoslovakia to surrender to German control, and made Bohemia and Moravia into a German "protectorate." As well as suffering the day-to-day brutalities of the German occupation, the citizens were also required to show a clear genealogy from the year 1600 onwards, to prove their racial purity, to the invaders who were now in control of their land and their destiny. Thankfully the townsfolk of historic and long-settled places like Brusperk didn't find this the impossible task that many of us might.

Sylvia got out just as Hitler was knocking at the door. She arrived in America in March 1938, and travelled almost immediately to Louisville, Kentucky. It was while she was working in the hospital there, in 1943, that she met medical Student John Doerr. His girl had stood him up, and he was in need of a date. Sylvia obliged, and before long things got serious. Once 1944 arrived, and John received his diploma and had taken his boards, they were married, (the very next day, in fact).

America was subject to gas and food rationing during World War Two, and John and Sylvia fell foul of this system due to administrative difficulties. John desired an army career like his father, and had studied at Medical School through the early years of the war on Reserve Officer basis. Disappointment awaited, as he was turned down on medical grounds. However, the Navy were keen to have him, and they requested that he resign his army commission, in order that he be free to accept a Navy one.

John was delighted with this prospect, although somewhat worried about his family's tendency towards severe seasickness. It will be remembered that both his Scottish grandmother and grandfather were very seasick during their emigration. His mother and father also found that they suffered from the same malady, when they had to ship out to the Philippines, back in 1909.

John's other problem was that his records got lost for three months, as the army attempted to pass him to the navy. This was a fairly big problem in wartime, because, during this period of rationing, food points and gas coupons – no records; no income. However, he and Sylvia worked at the same hospital, and were able to eat there, while on shift. Family helped too, because John's mother, Bessie, and her sisters, Mary and Jessie, all saved points and gas coupons for John and Sylvia to use during this time.

John became a transport surgeon, for some months before the war ended. His greatest joy, at this time, was that he seemed not to have inherited the dreaded seasickness gene. In fact, he says that working on the converted grain ship that had nineteen hundred troops onboard kept him too busy to even think of being seasick. They were stationed in the North Pacific, or Bering Sea, and it was always cold.

John and Sylvia's first child, John Allison Doerr, arrived in 1945. It was for him, and for any future siblings he might have, that John Charles began ordering all of his genealogical information. And now here I was, benefiting in a big way from the Scottish filing cabinets. I was able to copy documents, letters, and old photographs, which have all contributed to this overall tale. I also saw Sheriff John's shooting medals, and his battalion cup, and I held his Colt 38 Special.

I stayed only one day and night in Columbus, but what a fruitful time it was. Afterwards I travelled on, into the Great Smokies, and visited Cherokee. This is the only Indian Reservation east of the Mississippi River. Known as the Qualla Boundary, it houses the eastern portion of the Cherokee Nation. The rest of the Cherokee people were led west, on the Trail of Tears, by Chief John Ross. I was interested to learn what I could, of "Duyuktv" – the way of balance. There are close parallels with tribal clan culture in the Scottish Highlands, pre-Culloden.

I had also wanted to see Grandfather Mountain Highland Games Field. Sadly this was the one part of my trip that fell apart, due to the capricious nature of the weather. My guide, and font of North Carolinian knowledge, Ed Ingle, told me that if we had bad snow at Asheville altitude, then Grandfather Mountain wasn't happening. This wasn't all bad, because it gives an excuse to return when the Games are actually on, and see the site in it's full glory. The other upside was that Ed recommended, as a substitute itinerary for the day, looking at Kings Mountain Battlefield in South Carolina. (see Appendix I).

I finished that day, (Saint Patrick's Day), by passing the car back to the hire company in Charlotte, with some relief. I then booked into my hotel, and went out on the town. I was taken to be Irish on more than one occasion that night, but didn't want to make anyone feel foolish, so I didn't deny it. A good night was had by all.

The next morning saw me flying south, out of snow, and into the sunshine of Florida. The weather was marvellous when I landed at Tampa. I was staying with Wayne and Lynn Shelton at Bradenton. Wayne is an insurance adjustor, and thus the recent series of hurricanes to hit Florida is very much a conversation topic in their house. These events are even more personal too, because Lynn's parents, Norma and Andy, were badly hit by Hurricane Jeanne last September. Lynn's mother, Norma, is daughter to Old John's youngest son Edwin. (If that sounds a little complex, then clarification is available on the family chart on page 189).

Lynn was delighted when she heard that I was to be visiting them last. She realised immediately that this meant that she would get to hear all the tales that I had gathered, as I meandered back and forth across the USA.

Norma and Andy came over, from the Atlantic Coast, for a couple of days bringing another of those marvellous boxes full of photographs and documents. Lynn also had a large, and arresting portrait of her Grandfather, Old John Allison of Morrow. This portrait had been painted by an itinerant painter – one of the kind who would travel the backroads of America, offering to paint the pictures of these rural farmers in return for modest payment, and bed and board while the job was being done. The painter would have a variety of body-types already painted, would choose the best one, and then paint the subject's head! With the addition of this portrait, I had now collected good photographs of four of the original generation of Allison brothers. One final conversation that I was privileged to be part of was a discussion between Lynn, and Norma, her mother, about American Patchwork. A major tradition, in the States, has been for the women to make patchwork quilts representing the path of their lives. Lynn is aware of plenty of these, from prior generations, on her father's side, but not on her mother's side. Norma confirmed that fact, but also admitted that she didn't know why there was such an absence.

This was an issue close to Lynn's heart, as she is particularly skilled and interested in fabrics and soft furnishing works. However, once a lack is identified, it's all the easier to address.

On a different, but related topic, I had decided not to take my kilt to America with me. I made this decision mostly on the basis of how much internal travelling I would be doing, and space available in my luggage. However, my kilt is Allison tartan, and I thought that all of these Allison relations might like to at least see what Allison tartan looks like. So I made a contact sheet of nine photographs of my kilt, and took this with me instead.

As we spoke of the absence of patchwork quilts among the Allison descendants Lynn suddenly became very energised. Brandishing the image of the Allison tartan, she announced "I could get hold of a bolt of this cloth, and create some fine items for the Allison heritage"

Walter Allison (1825 – 1903).

John Allison (1831 – 1928).

James Allison (1844 – 1925)
holding John C. Doerr, 1918.

David Allison (1846 – 1935).

Now that I'm home, on the eastern side of the Atlantic Ocean, we are trying to make that happen. It's not a substitute for the patchwork. It's something different. But it's equally rich and deep, and will hopefully endure, down through the generations yet to come.

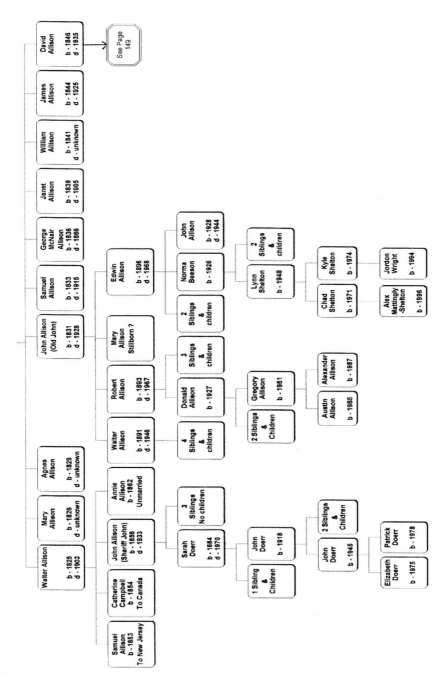

Allison brothers, Walter and John – some selected American descendants of John and Edie Allison (1831 to the present), and some selected descendants of John's elder brother, Walter.

Chapter Eleven

The Weaving of Warp and Weft

"Hauf his soul a Scot maun use
Indulgin' in illusions;
And hauf in getting' rid o' them,
And comin' to conclusions."
Hugh MacDiarmid

The Abercorn Bar was busy. People were arriving to see the band. It was the late 1970's, and I was waiting to see my older brother, William. He was Road Manager for "The Freeze", who were due to arrive here any minute. I was studying at Glasgow University, and I didn't see him often, so this was a rare opportunity. There is little else to this incident, and yet it leads us to some entertaining speculation.

As far as I know, neither of us had ever been in Paisley before. Certainly, neither of us knew about the medieval drain, just across the road, at Paisley Abbey, waiting to be discovered more than a decade in the future. Did we know of our own links to the burgh, or its history as a major textile centre? I think not. Yet here was a town which had featured strongly in our family's story, and in Scotland's too. At that point we were standing too close to the pattern to see the weave. And yet the Warp and Weft were all around us, coaxing us into the tangle that is past, present and future.

The previous three chapters described the lives of people in Scotland, Australia, and America in turn. This chapter considers questions of heritage, tradition, and legend, together with the fragility of knowledge, and the incidence of the inexplicable.

Scots have ever been travellers, traders, soldiers, and sailors. Where they went, and what they did, is well documented, in a wide range of excellent history books. This body of work is a precious gift, and helps us to better understand the past. Where things unravel, however, is when history is used to try to help us make sense of the present. How people behave, and the choices they make are determined at least as much by heritage as by history.

Pick a bookshop, any bookshop, and you will find that books on heritage are generally in much shorter supply than books on history. Nonetheless, there are a few fine books on the topic, and better yet, a few of these deal directly with heritage as it affects Scottish emigrants. Perhaps the most in-depth coverage which I have found is in Celeste Ray's book – "Highland Heritage – Scottish Americans in the American South". However, I have also been fortunate to work with up-and-coming talent, such as Catriona Vernal, a student at Glasgow University, whose final year dissertation is an investigation into the roles that culture and heritage play in the American–Scottish relationship.

Celeste Ray provides a good working definition of heritage, and it's relative value:

> *"The value of heritage lies in it's perennial flexibility and the strength of the emotions it evokes. Celebratory and commemorative reflections on ancestral experience . . . interpret a past in a form meaningful for a particular group or individual at a particular . . . time.* (These events do this by merging historical incidents, folk memories, selected traditions and often sheer fantasy). *The bits of the past that seem most significant continuously change relative to the present."*

She also reminds us of the importance of the place of heritage in current affairs:

> *"Because visions of heritage most commonly alter and even distort history in appealing ways, what we perceive as heritage replaces history and becomes our memory . . . For the individual, and for collectives such as ethnic groups or nations,*

public memory charters action in the present. This alone should cause us to contemplate the ways in which history metamorphoses into heritage".

One example, given to me by John Wilson from Texas, is that of the Scots from Wilson County, Tennessee. Until well after the the beginning of the Twentieth Century young people had play parties. These were generally held in the winter, at various homes, and were performed to the singing of ditties. One was called "Weeviley Wheat". It didn't differ particularly from any of the others. Some of the lines ran:

> *"I'll have none of your weeviley wheat*
> *And I'll have none of your barley!*
> *I'll take a little of your good old rye*
> *And make a cake for Charlie."*

When this was sung, the girls dropped out. They didn't know why. Nice girls just didn't play "Weeviley Wheat" and, if they did, they knew what would happen to them when they got home. The reality was that this was the old Cavalier song, "Over the Water to Charlie." It originated when the Stuarts were in exile, in France. Of course, it was anathema to the Puritans. These Wilson County girls of Puritan extraction did not know all of this. They were almost 10 generations, an ocean, and half a continent away from it all. And yet, when "Weevily Wheat" was sung, they walked righteously out of the game and sat down.

Heritage, then, is sometimes rooted in what an individual or group perceive to be their history, and can also be related to forgotten history. But more complicated than that, heritage is heavily affected by the present day. Our day-to-day beliefs, and our politics both colour how we see the past. Heritage is also dynamic. It can change, or develop, to accommodate changes in society. Sometimes new "traditions" arise, complete with a perceived background.

This concept of ideas going out to other lands carried by the rivers of emigrants is what first sparked my interest in heritage. While working at Culloden Battlefield, I became increasingly aware of significant numbers of North Americans asking the way to "The Well of the Dead". When I asked as to the reason, they said that they required to "dip their bonnets" there, as a mark of respect. This wasn't something that native Scots indulged in, and so I enquired further. I was told that this tradition began at the Battle of Killiecrankie, with a toast in a bonnet, and later evolved into toasting the "King over the water". It was explained to me that the Jacobites had always had this association with water, and so the combination of the bonnet, and the dipping in the well, was a suitable mark of respect for the dead.

I found this fascinating, and I began following up the idea of traditions going out with emigrants, changing through time, and coming back to us as something else. I also looked, with some success, for new traditions which had evolved with the emigrants.

North Carolina is a particularly fruitful place in which to search for evidence of evolving traditions. My ever-helpful guide, Ed Ingle, was able to tell me about the "christening" of a new kilt, by dropping a little whisky on it. We also encountered the blessing of new sgian dubhs, (kilt-sock knives), and heard about the "Kirkin' o' the Tartan". This event involves the banners of clan tartans being paraded forward through a church.

By far the biggest, and most visible new Scottish tradition is America's Tartan Day. It was established as a national celebration of the contribution made by Scots and latter day Scots-Americans to the foundation, character and prosperity of the United States of America.

Tartan Day is a Senate approved holiday. Senate Resolution 155 states that "April 6th has a special significance for all Americans, and especially those Americans of Scottish descent, because the Declaration of Arbroath, the Scottish Declaration of Independence, was signed on April 6th, 1320 and the American Declaration of Independence was modelled on that inspirational document". So it can be seen that Tartan Day is, (on a very big scale), a fine example of the use of real, and historically significant dates to give added value to the development of heritage celebration and tradition.

Heritage and history are an ever-present background, at a place like Culloden Battlefield too. During my time on the public counter at

Culloden, I have been privileged to witness the range of differing relationships and reactions by which our visitors interact with the site.

For the purposes of this tale of Rivers Running Far, I am particularly interested in how Americans and Australians view Culloden. Huge numbers of both nationalities wend their way towards the Battlefield, when in Britain. This is mainly due to the iconic nature of the site.

The field at Culloden resonates very strongly for Americans, bringing more of them every day, seeking information about the battle and those who fought in it. Many prisoners were shipped to America and Antigua after the battle. In addition to those forcibly shipped, others with Jacobite sympathies fled to America, during the decades, both before, and after, the 1745 Rising.

The centuries, however, have provided many other reasons for emigration, as we have already seen. Yet these other causes don't have the same hold on the heart and psyche of the Scots-American. Why is that? I believe that the answer to this question lies in the difference between heritage and history.

The Scots heritage revival in America began in the American South, in the 1950's. Heritage Revival is often prompted by feelings that something has been lost or taken, and has to be reclaimed. In this case, the mythology surrounds the loss of clan culture and homeland, following Culloden. This "romance of the lost cause" was immensely powerful and attractive for Southerners, given that they already had their own version of a glorious lost cause provided by Robert E Lee, and the Confederacy. Although this revival began in the south, it later spread across the nation, as ancestral and ethnic issues grabbed the country's imagination.

The American bicentennial celebrations, and the success of Alex Haley's book, Roots, have both fuelled the interest that Americans have in ethnic identity. Catriona Vernal proposes that ideas of equality, belonging, and community are pivotal to such an ethnic revival. She feels that the Scottish ethnic identity in particular has been extremely capable of providing these requirements. It also provides continuity with the past, and a level of uniqueness within general American culture.

With the nation eagerly taking to genealogy, it wasn't long before all of the trappings of the "Lost Cause" mythology, complete with Parades, and Highland Games, spread throughout the rest of the States. This then explains the place of Culloden in the American heart.

Some emigrants moved on from North America, to settle, finally, in the Antipodes instead. The most famous of these were Reverend Norman MacLeod, (a Presbyterian minister), together with his congregation of several hundred people. They had already emigrated from the Highlands of Scotland to Cape Breton Island, in 1817. The onset of the potato famine, almost thirty years later, in 1845, caused terrible deprivation in Cape Breton, and set Norman MacLeod on his travels again.

He is quoted as saying "The general destitution has made it impossible, even for the most saving, to shut their ears and eyes from the alarming claims and craving of those around them, running continually from door to door, with the ghastly features of death staring in their very faces". These appalling conditions were the main factor in the flock's decision to pack up and follow the Reverend Norman first to Australia, and then ultimately, on to Waipu, in New Zealand.

They were not the only party to do this. There are numerous other examples. While I was in Monto, in Queensland, I drove north out of town to visit Max and Lynn, who own the Waratah Winery. I spoke to Lynn at the Vineyard, and later tracked Max Lindsay down, at the Mungungo Pub. He confirmed that his own emigrant ancestor had gone first to Canada. Things did not go well however, and before long he was on his way to Australia, because, as he put it – "It's better to starve to death in a warm climate!"

Culloden is a pilgrimage site for Australians too. Although Australia wasn't settled until decades after the battle, many Australians whose ancestors were displaced by the Highland Clearances view Culloden as the single causal event leading to those Clearances. Thus when they come here (to the ancestral homeland) a visit to Culloden is seen as an essential part of the programme. That's because it's usually easier for people to identify with one place and one event, rather than with a range of complex political, economic, or sociological ideas.

I was fascinated by the story in a letter which I received, in May 2004 , from one of my Australian relatives. Don Minto doesn't live in the centre of any of the major cities in Australia. He lives just south of Brisbane, in Logan City, Queensland. Given the suburban location, it was a surprise to read about the following event:

> *"You may be interested to know that a few weeks ago, I went with two of my old mates to our regular monthly "meeting" at a tavern in a large shopping center near home. There is a town square within the shopping center right next to the tavern and there were all these people dressed in strange costumes "fighting" each other with swords and pipers galore. My mates and I wondered what was going on but did not enquire as to the reason for the noise etc. It was not until I got back home that I realized that it must have been for the Battle of Culloden anniversary".*

Culloden is not the only icon held within the hearts of the descendants of emigrant Scots. I discovered an interesting clutch of icons and traditions, on both the continents I visited. New Year celebrations and First Footing were high on the agenda, but so were stovies, whisky, "Oor Wullie", and potted meat. Other things that were seen as Scottish included tartan, landscape, bagpipes, heather and beer.

The twentieth century has been a difficult period through which to keep knowledge and traditions alive. It brought us a global flu epidemic, two world wars, consumerism and humanity's soporific – the television. Given all these, we have probably done well to retain as many stories as we have.

My own father is a good example of how the twentieth century impacted badly on family knowledge. This storehouse of lore is fragile, and depends on the survival of family members, to pass it on. My father always maintained that he had no Australian relatives. This situation remained unchanged until one day in the 1980's, when they came knocking at the door!

The problem was that his mother, Ruth Minto, had died when he was still only six years old. Ruth's brother, (Robert), had predeceased her in 1917, killed in the first world war, and her sister, (Mary), had died in the 1918 flu epidemic. By the time my father was old enough to be curious, both his Minto grandparents had also passed on. It is therefore no real surprise that he was unaware of George and Agnes' emigration in 1911, and knew nothing of their descendants making a life for themselves, in Australia.

In a similar vein, the very human and tragic tale of John Allison's military career with the British army was unknown by his own descendants until the 1970's. John had told all of his children that he emigrated on a three-masted ship, out of Edinburgh.

This is a perfectly understandable attempt to legitimise his position, and afford the family some dignity. In reality, I think that his decision to leave the disease-ridden army posting behind him was a perfectly reasonable one.

The story came to light when John Charles Doerr visited us in Scotland late in the 1970's. My father was well aware of the circumstances surrounding John Allison's emigration, as it was his father, (my own grandfather), who had written to the war office seeking a pardon, back in 1910. Although the background all came as a surprise for John Doerr, he nonetheless accepted the story as a credible tale. Furthermore, he was able to add to it, due to his knowledge of the medical history of Bermuda. It was he who put names to the likely fevers sweeping the barracks at that time – plague, or perhaps cholera?

Both of these examples show how easy it is for knowledge to be lost – either through the loss of those who carry the information, or sometimes even by the deliberate actions of those who have reason to alter a story. Of course, the opposite of this happens too. This is what I call "the apple effect", when the most wonderful stories and facts fall straight into your outstretched hand just when you least expect it. One instance of this was when I found myself sharing that evening with Robert Fraser Dodd, (see page 158), and learned, first-hand, all about his ancestor, Alexander, the Bonnymuir Uprising insurgent.

In May 2004 I was participating in Nairn Book Week, and found myself in Nairn Library, delivering a presentation on writing. I had just explained the "apple effect" and illustrated it by the Bonnymuir story, when it happened again.

The Weaving of Warp and Weft

One lady in the company questioned whether such information was likely to drop into the hand, if one left it too late to begin looking. She explained how her grandparents died young, (when her mother was only five), and her only relative with knowledge of that side of the family was an Australian uncle. I suggested that he might be a source of information. She sorrowfully replied that she had left it too long.

Now that she herself was getting on, the uncle had died. No-one would be likely to know much about him, as he had been a sea-faring man out of Sydney. I told her not to lose heart, and as an example, said that some of my most interesting information was about someone in similar situation – a relative of mine who was a Sydney Sea-Captain. She asked the name, and as I replied Captain Thomas Minto, everyone in the room saw her lose colour, and then flush, as she cried "They knew each other. More than that. My uncle was Captain Gibson. Captain Minto was his business partner"

This was the "apple effect" at it's best. Stories and opportunities presenting themselves when least expected, and offering new connections and access to information where people had previously thought that there were none. All the better that this particular apple had dropped in front of a roomful of interested readers, and that they may, in turn, be encouraged to undertake research into their own families.

Coincidences such as these are not uncommon, as one follows the tangled threads of family research. There is a feeling that nature, itself, is working within the weave. Nature usually tries to re-establish patterns, but faced with humanity's riotous disorder, in this case has to be content with teasing us through coincidence, and the inexplicable.

In my journeys across America, names seemed to be a recurrent theme. Even the families who had become isolated from family knowledge were giving their children family names, (like Alexander), without ever knowing the connection. Two of my relatives who had never previously met each other, discovered in March 2005, that the granddaughter of one, and daughter of the other, shared the same sequence of names, only transposed.

Places and landscapes can also contribute a strange story or two. When I first contacted Greg Allison in Ohio, I asked if he had always lived in Morrow. The answer was no. He had, in fact, moved there relatively recently. He, and his wife Angela, were looking to buy property, and could really have bought anywhere in the United States. However, they viewed one piece of land that they felt immediately drawn to. It sang to them, and they said that they loved it, right away. They bought it, and subsequently built their house on it. It was when Greg's father came to call that everything became clear. He stood outside, looking thoughtful for a while, and then announced "This is part of your Uncle Ed's Farm" Greg, all unknowing, and never having previously visited it, had bought back a piece of the family history!

When I visited Australia, the date 1911 repeated on me constantly. It was the date that George and Agnes emigrated. It was also, however, the date on the painting in Brisbane Museum which best illustrated turn-of-the-century living. When I was taken to the top of Mount Coot-tha, the interpretive boards showed a panorama of Brisbane, in 1911. When I went north to Jambin, I enjoyed a drive around Kurrajong in the Shannons' perfectly restored Napier car – originally built in 1911. Back south again, I found an excellent book on early Australia. It's publication date was 1911. I saw a postcard in Sydney, of the city skyline, as it was, when? Yes, 1911. There were other instances, too, but these are probably sufficient to convey the theme.

The final collection of true tales which I gathered, while in Australia, are what I have called "the clock stories". At least four branches of the family have strange clock tales. Taken together, they make a full set of the inexplicable, so here they are, in the words of the tellers themselves:

Reg's Clock

The grandfather clock which stands in the corner of my lounge room today, manufactured circa 1830, has been in the Minto family for an undetermined period. It still operates and I wind it up at least once each week with a large brass winder. The leaden weights are

Reg's Clock.

shockingly heavy. The cabinet is made of cheap pine wood and varnished. It has never been restored and shows signs of long extinct wood borers. It just kept running.

I do not know it's history. It is handed down from father to eldest son by tradition. I believe that the clock did not come to Australia with the family on the "Otway" but was forwarded later when they moved in to their new home. It is alleged that it was sent along with a couple of paintings . . . It is also alleged that the paintings were disposed of to meet the duty on the clock. One can only assume that the clock . . . meant much to them for them to bear the cost of shipping it to Australia.

Due to the cheap construction of the cabinet, my dad used to jokingly say – "Maybe we should break the weights apart. We might find them full of gold sovereigns, (perhaps the Minto fortune), as surely nobody would pay all that money to ship an old and cheaply made clock so far over the sea".

Tom's Clock Part One (dated 29th August 1995)

It was given to Celia and myself as a wedding present by my brother Adam in 1938. It chimed every quarter hour and struck the hours 1 to 12. It was activated by springs.

201

About 1989 it started to give trouble . . . I moved it to the bedroom. You cannot sleep with a Chiming Clock so I no longer wound the Chimes or the Hour Strike.

Celia died before breakfast on the 27th August 1991. It was in the bedroom and very sudden. On the fourth anniversary of her death, 27th August 1995, I was making the bed and thinking of her. The time was 7.20am (not the time for the clock to strike the hour). I was two metres from the clock. It struck 12 times. Yes, 12 times.

Makes you wonder, does it not . . . I will let you know if the clock strikes again.

Tom's Clock Part Two (dated 18th February 1996)

Henry Minto, a second cousin from Vancouver, Canada recently made a first contact and . . . he and his wife were to visit me on Thursday 15th Feb 1996. As a consequence I had been looking through old family albums and sorted out a number of photographs. The date was 10th Feb 1996.

At 9.04am Sydney Summer time 12th Feb 1996 I was in the bedroom standing about one metre from the clock and thinking about nothing in particular. The Clock commenced to strike 13 times, Yes 13 times.

As it is now approaching six years since the Chimes were last wound . . . I put the inexplicable down to my activity with the photographs. At 6am next morning I woke suddenly, with the thought that Celia's birthday was in February. Double-checking her passport yielded the details Date of Birth-Port, Glasgow, 11th Feb, 1915.

9.04 am Sydney summer time, 12th Feb 1996 is 10.04pm, 11th Feb 1996 British time. I must check Celia's Birth Certificate (at the bank) to see if it gives time of birth!

Alan's Clock

Tom and Celia Minto gave Alan and Phyllis Minto a clock as a wedding gift and vice versa. (Uncle Tom's Clock story is about the clock that

Alan and Phyllis had given them). Phyllis had a stroke at 3:05pm on the Wednesday 11th 1999 and passed away on the 13th. On Tuesday 17th the clock was packed away in a box and placed in the middle of the lounge room. It had not been wound on. The following day while Joan and Alan were packing things in boxes on the 18th August, exactly one week after Phyllis had taken the stroke, the clock started chiming. Joan immediately looked at the time and noticed it was 3.05pm. the same time as Phyllis had had the stroke one week earlier.

Joan's Clock

My clock was left to me by my parents. It was originally one of George and Agnes' wedding presents, and had been brought out on the ship from Scotland. During alterations to my home in March 2001, the key to the clock was misplaced, and hence the clock has not been wound since that time. On 4.1.04, (My eldest daughter's birthday), we were entertaining friends, Peter Richards and his partner Bev. For a time, conversation centred around our parents, (all deceased), and our sisters, (also deceased). We got up from the table, and the clock struck. I was in too much shock to tell you how many times, but the time was 10.20pm, the time on the clock was 9.00, and it went for 12 minutes. My husband Cliff made the comment that if he had not been a witness he definitely would not have believed us. The clock had not been bumped, moved, or touched!

We have seen traditions that have travelled out, around the world, that are still practiced today. We have also seen new traditions which have developed to fulfil certain given requirements. And finally we have looked carefully at the legendary, the co-incidental, and the downright inexplicable. All of this, taken together with the fact of how easy it is to lose knowledge of our family branches, is like a riotous jumbling of the warp and the weft.

But it *is* possible to get hold of the loom, and to help nature to reweave the order back into some of the pattern. Celeste Ray says that:

"In pursuit of heritage the genealogist collects lives with a mission : restoring the legacies of forgotten or half-remembered generations establishes one's own legacy. Informants say that providing those in the future with some of the past gives a satisfying completeness to one's own life and secures one's own place in history."

Two of the most satisfying events for me, as this book came together, were meals, attended by members of branches of the family who had been out of contact with each other for a century and more.

The first of these was at Alison Stasa's house, at Carlingford, in Sydney, in March 2004. Alison is Tom Minto's daughter, (see table, page 169). I first hinted at this meeting, on page 143. I explained, on that page, that the descendants of my great-grandfather Thomas' eldest brother, (Henry), had emigrated to Canada. Henry's great-granddaughter, Adele, met and married an Australian, Mark Howse. They now live in Sydney, and made contact with the Sydney Mintos not long before my visit. It was inspired of Alison to think to invite both Adele and I to lunch, before I left Australia.

We, all of us, talked for hours – the descendants of those three brothers, Henry, Thomas, and George, reunited for the first time since 1911.

I had a similar experience in America a year later. This was at a meal in the Golden Lamb, Lebanon, Ohio. I was there with Kathy Williams, who is the great-granddaughter of Old John Allison from Morrow. Meeting us was Debbie Coleman and her daughter Allison. Debbie is the great-great-great-granddaughter of Walter Allison, (see table, page 189). Kathy and Debbie had never met before, being from such widely divergent branches of the family. Yet here we were, probably for the first time since John had left Renfrewshire to join in the Army, in about 1850. Representatives of each of the brothers, in the same room at the same time, chatting -Debbie descending from Walter, the eldest brother. Kathy descending from John, and me descending from David, the youngest of them all.

At events like these it's easy to feel the truth of the concept that we are reweaving the threads that bind the past with the present, for the benefit of those in the future.

These travels through both Australia and America were enormously inspirational. I met so many special people, all of whom were so happy to share their tales and stories. But much more than this, I was able to revel in the visiting of places that I had only imagined, through all the years of my growing. In a way, this was different from the kind of heritage pilgrimage that descendants of emigrants make, when they return to this, their ancestral homeland. Yet my journey still had the feeling of an ancestry quest. I was following those Rivers that had flowed out from Scotland, and I was mapping their course, as they ran blithely into the future.

Those places which I visited had long occupied a place in my mind, and I had many times visualised what it might be like to walk down the street in Monto, Queensland, or sit on John Allison's porch in Morrow, Ohio. These places, for me, were as much part of the "Legendary Landscape" as places like Culloden and Bannockburn are, for the ancestral pilgrims who come back to Scotland.

In finding and walking in these places I felt the truth of the assertion made by Celeste Ray, regarding the importance of landscape to the celebration and experiencing of heritage. She uses the Grandfather Mountain event to illustrate this:

"Participants claim the Scotland-like scene created on Grandfather Mountain allows them to feel transported to their spiritual home, to shut out the ordinary world and more easily remember and emplace their ancestors. As the clans annually converge on MacRae Meadows for the pre-games torchlight ceremony, an emcee sets the scene by asking participants to quietly "consider the mountain. It's strength and size shield us from the world beyond . . . Time starts to slow, we move to a different pulse, a different age . . . It is time to wonder, to remember . . . The blood calls . . . Be silent and listen to the old long since""

I listen, but what I hear is the sound of white-water. I hear it leaping, and churning, and foaming, as it tumbles through these legendary hills and glens. And everywhere is the euphoria of life, running round the next bend in the stream, and out into the wider world.

Clearing Skies

"Scotland is not a place, of course. It is a state of mind. Probably every country is and we should be cautious when we assume we are unique. Other people may be just as crazy as we are."
Cliff Hanley

The engine of the Toyota spacecruiser was barely audible, within the comfortable passenger compartment. So talking was easy, as the road swept through the endless forests of the east coast, and miles of New York State Thruway disappeared beneath the front wheels.

It was the year 2000, and I was working in the United States at the time. On this particular trip, (many hours in length), I was being driven by an American friend, and talk had turned to forebears. I told some stories of my ancestors, but when I asked my friend if they had similar tales, the answer was "No". The process of emigration had dislocated the normal support networks of extended family. My acquaintance was an only child, with no mother, and a father with major social problems, who never spoke of the past. There were no other family members. There was therefore no inherited knowledge of family background, no knowledge of their place of origin, no sense of ethnic community, and not even any knowledge of where to culturally fit, (i.e. whether German, Norse, Celtic, or other ancestry).

Interestingly, that kind of blank sheet origin brings with it both advantages and disadvantages. Having no "natal" culture removes a list of useful triggers which help us to automatically respond to a given situation. At the same time, however, it gives the strength and freedom to more easily transcend what might be seen to be the traditional role for someone from a given cultural or ethnic background. My friend was grateful of the opportunity for a start in life free of such preconceived paths, but at the same time saddened by feelings of rootlessness, which can accompany such circumstances.

By coincidence the other "somewhat deep" conversation I had, which set me on my present course was also when I was on a journey. Doubtless a psychologist could make much of that, but we'll keep our considerations simple for now. So here I was, in a car, and once again my front wheels were eating miles. But this time they were Lanarkshire miles, and I was with my wife. We were driving along the valley of the Garf Water, on the south side of Tinto Hill. We had been to find the old Plenderleith property of Sornfallow, and our minds were full of thoughts of Minto ancestry, and of genealogy generally.

We began by considering the fragility of the knowledge, (as has already been referred to, within these pages, in Chapter Eleven). Interest in family roots and in personal heritage waned significantly during the twentieth century, and, in part, that loss of interest paralleled the change in the way a person viewed their own identity. Increasingly, in a society fast turning to consumerism, identity was measured by wealth, and by possession of material goods, rather than by the knowledge of one's place in the land, and within the family.

Our discussion then turned to a review of the most recent global trends in ancestral research. Despite the decades during which identity by "Who" was sublimated by identity by "What", it seems that the importance of the "Who" was never wholly lost, and now seems to be rushing back with renewed strength.

This would seem to be the right time to tell a tale of Rivers Running Far. In times past, our Iron Age hunter would scent the air, to gauge what weather was on the way. Our modern equivalent would be to have a look at what is energising the world of commerce. And energising the world of commerce right now is the worldwide growth in ancestral tourism. As a result, a government-promoted partnership, the "Ancestral Tourism Industry Steering Group" was established here, to develop ancestral tourism in Scotland. This process is aimed at improving the quality of visitors' experience, while also encouraging businesses to tap into this growing market.

So this is our weathervane. When governments say "no business can afford to ignore genealogy – one of the world's fastest growing pastimes" then we know that a person's sense of identity, (their sense of self), is increasingly being set in terms of their relationships to their fellow man, rather than by their fiscal value, creed, or colour.

There has been a great outpouring of rivers of Scots across the globe, and they integrated and intermarried on every continent of the world. It is fascinating then, to consider one of life's small ironies. Although we might initially think that ancestral research creates ties that bind back to one ancestral homeland, the converse is also true. People of every colour and culture throughout the world carry names like Grant, Scott, MacDonald, and many others. Follow their family trees and they will take you in every imaginable direction, from Scot to Shawnee, and from Masai to Maori. Genealogy, therefore breaks down barriers, rather than creating them, and brings us closer to the ideal – "That man to man the world o'er, shall brithers be for a' that."

Cliff Hanley spoke truly, when he said " Scotland . . . is a state of mind." However, although Cliff calls for caution in any assumption that we are unique, which seems wise considering how well-stirred the world's pot has been, Robert Louis Stevenson is not altogether wrong when he identifies a particular Scottish trait thus:

> *"For that is the mark of the Scots of all classes:*
> *that he stands in an attitude towards the past*
> *unthinkable to Englishmen, and remembers and*
> *cherishes the memory of his forebears, good or*
> *bad; and there burns alive in him a sense of identity*
> *with the dead even to the twentieth generation."*

This sense of identity with previous generations is nurtured by our refusal to consider separation as having permanence. We outmanoeuvre permanence by grouping "those who came before" and "those who went away" in the same general category – and subjecting both to the promise "Gone, but not forgotten". The difference is that the emigrant is still around to take up the invite . . .

"The door is open, and the kettle is on. Come away in!"

And so our tale is done, and all that remains is to offer a little advice that I, myself, have patently ignored, as I led you through these pages of water-based metaphor . . .

"Don't quote your proverb until you bring your ship into port"
from the Gaelic

Appendices

Appendix 1

The Overmountain Men
(adapted from NPS literature)

These men came from the northern slopes of the Appalachian Mountains, from the area now known as Tennessee. Most were of Scots-Irish ancestry, now living in the valleys around the headwaters of the Holston, Nolichucky, and Watauga rivers. Years earlier they had established settlements that were remote and nearly independent of royal authority, and they numbered many Allisons among them. They were fiercely self-reliant, with little concern for the war being fought in the northern colonies and along the coast.

When Charleston, South Carolina, surrendered to the British army, May 12th 1780, the British captured most of the Continental troops in the South. Only patriot militia remained, to oppose a British move through North Carolina into Virginia, America's largest colony. Lord Cornwallis appointed Major Patrick Ferguson to recruit a force of loyalists to defeat the local militia. As Ferguson campaigned across the Carolina upcountry that summer, some frontier patriots came over the mountains to aid their compatriots. It was then that Ferguson made his fatal mistake.

He sent a message to Issac Shelby, leader of the Overmountain men. He threatened to march into the mountains and "lay waste the country with fire and sword" if they did not lay down their arms, and pledge allegiance to the King.

They came, but full of righteous wrath. A furious army of Overmountain men gathered at Sycamore Shoals, Tennessee, and began an arduous march through the snowy mountains. Growing in numbers as they marched east, some 900 men gave chase to Ferguson, surrounding his army on Kings Mountain, South Carolina. In a little over an hour, they killed or captured his entire command.

Thomas Jefferson described the victory as "That Turn of the Tide of Success."

Appendix II

Highland Oatmeal Breakfast Pancakes
A Recipe

Ingredients:

2 heaped dessert spoons of oatmeal
1 heaped dessertspoon flour
A little milk
Salt, pepper and herbs

- Mix the dry ingredients in a bowl – oats, flour, salt, pepper, and mixed herbs.

- Add enough milk to make a thinnish batter.

- Heat a little oil in frying-pan first, and then drop spoonfuls of batter into the pan.

- Fry (turning as necessary) until golden both sides.

Of course, for al fresco Australian picnics in public parks, involving about thirty people, multiplying the above ingredients by a factor of ten would be a good idea – as is finding a hot cooking plate with no central hole. Feeding the Chef with reasonable quantities of Castlemaine Gold works well too.

Appendix III

I Want To Go To Morrow

I started on a journey just about a week ago,
For a little town of Morrow, in the state of Ohio,
I never was a traveller, and really didn't know,
That Morrow had been ridiculed a century ago,
I went down to the depot for my ticket and applied
For the tips regarding Morrow, not expecting to be guyed.
Said I, "My friend, I want to go to Morrow and return
Not later than tomorrow, for I haven't time to burn."
Said he to me, "Now let me see if I have heard you right.
You want to go to Morrow and back tomorrow night.
You should have gone to Morrow yesterday and back today,
For if you started yesterday to Morrow, don't you see,
You could have got to Morrow and return today at three.
The train that started yesterday – now understand me right –
Today it gets to Morrow, and returns tomorrow night."
Said I, "My boy, it seems to me you're talking through your hat,
Is there a town named Morrow on your line? Now tell me that."
"There is," said he, "and take from me a quiet little tip –
To go from here to Morrow is the time of a fourteen trip.
The train that goes to Morrow leaves today, eight-thirty-five;
Half after ten tomorrow is the time it should arrive,
Now if from here to Morrow is a fourteen hour jump,
Can you go today to Morrow and come back today chump?"
Said I , "I want to go to Morrow; can I go today
And get to Morrow tonight, if there is no delay?"
"Well, well," said he, "explain to me and I've no more to say:
Can you go anywhere tomorrow and come back today?
For if you'd get to Morrow; surely you agree
You should have started not today, but yesterday, you see.

So if you start to Morrow, leaving here today, you're flat,
You won't get to Morrow till the day that follows that.
Now if you start today to Morrow, it's a cinch you'll land
Tomorrow into Morrow, not today you understand.
For the train today to Morrow, if the schedule is right,
Will get you into Morrow by about tomorrow night."
Said I, "Guess you know it all, but kindly let me say,
How can I go to Morrow if I leave the town today?"
Said he, "You cannot go to Morrow any more today,
For the train that goes to Morrow is a mile upon it's way."

I was so disappointed I was mad enough to swear;
The train had gone to Morrow and had left me standing there.
The man was right in telling me I was a howling jay;
I didn't go to Morrow, so I guess I'll go today.

Appendix IV

Obituary for John Edgar Allison
(Johnnie)

John Edgar Allison, son of Edwin and Margaret Ludlum Allison, was born in the Ludlum ancestral homestead near Morrow, Ohio, June 21st, 1928, and departed this life at Blair Brothers Hospital, Lebanon, Ohio on June 4th, 1944. Aged 15 years, 11 months, 13 days, Johnnie, as he was called, by his classmates and others, was a true son of the soil, his principal interest was the development and improvement of his Grandfather Ludlum's farm. From childhood he assisted with the farm work and at an early age was entrusted by his parents with a considerable portion of the farm duties. Johnnie was at his happiest when his tasks were the most difficult and when he could lend a hand towards helping his neighbours.

Johnnie attended Morrow High School and was in the Sophomore year at the time of his parting. His many school friends will miss his jovial manner, broad smile, and sympathetic understanding. During his Sophomore year in school he was especially active in all salvage and bond drives, giving of his time and energy, after the chores on the farm were finished, thus showing the true spirit of patriotism.

Though his years on this earth were few, he had learned completely the lessons of thrift, industry, and compassion. His reverence for his parents, brother and sisters was one of his principal tenets. We are grateful for his gentleness and tenderness, for his deep sympathy and human kindness : though he is gone from us his spirit endures with us.

He leaves to Mourn him his parents, one brother Ralph, his sisters, Dorothy and Norma, his grandfather and grandmother Ludlum, several aunts and uncles and cousins, and his many friends.

"You, my son,

Have shown me God,

Your Kiss upon my cheek

Has made me feel the gentle

touch

of him who leads us on.

The memory of yor smile,

When young,

Reveals his face,

As mellowing years

Come on apace.

And when you went before,

you left the gates of heaven ajar

That I may glimpse,

Approaching from afar,

The glories of his grace.

Hold, son, my hand.

Guide me along the path

That, coming,

I may stumble not,

Nor roam,

Nor fail to see the way

Which leads us home."

Bibliography

Anderson, Ian G., *Scotsmen In The Service of The Czars*, Pentland Press, Haddington, 1990.

Anderson, Marjorie O., *Kings and Kingship in Early Scotland*, Scottish Academic Press, Edinburgh, 1973.

Ascherson, Neal, *Stone Voices*, Granta Books, London, 2002.

Ashley, Mike, *British Kings and Queens*, Barnes and Noble Inc., New York, 1998.

Blainey, Geoffrey, *Black Kettle and Full Moon*, Penguin, Australia, 2003.

Boardman, Stephen, *The Early Stewart Kings*, Tuckwell Press, East Linton, 1996.

Boswell, James, *The Journal of a Tour to the Hebrides*, Penguin, London, 1984.

Bower, Walter, *A History Book For Scots*, University of St Andrews, St. Andrews, 1998.

Calder Jenni, *Scots in Canada*, Luath Press, Edinburgh, 2003.

Campbell, Marion, *Argyll*, Colin Baxter, Grantown-On-Spey, 1995.

Chetcuti, Jim, *Expressions of Australia*, Australia "thru the lens", 2003.

Coombe, Mark, *A Day in the Outback*, Mark Coombe, 2002.

Crane, Stephen, *The Red Badge of Courage*, The Folio Society, London, 1951.

Cruden, Stewart, *The Scottish Castle*, Spurbooks, Edinburgh, 1960.

Devine, T.M., *The Scottish Nation 1700–2000*, Penguin, London, 1999.

Dickinson, W. Croft, *Scotland from the Earliest Times to 1603*, Oxford University Press, Oxford, 1977.

Donaldson, Professor Gordon, *Scottish Historical Documents*, Neil Wilson Publishing, Glasgow, Post 1993.

Ganeri, Anita with **Martell, Hazel Mary** and **Williams, Brian**, *World History Encyclopedia*, Parragon, Bath, 2001.

Gies, Frances and **Joseph**, *Daily Life in Medieval Times*, Black Dog and Leventhal Publishers, New York, 1990.

Gratzer, Walter, *The Undergrowth of Science*, Oxford University Press, 2000.

Grimble, Ian, *Clans and Chiefs*, Barnes and Noble, New York, 1980.

Handlin, Oscar, *The American People*, Penguin Books, London, 1966.

Highland Destitution Records: ex HD6/1. *Report on the Western Highlands and Islands*, 1851, minutes of evidence, p73.

Houston, R. A. and **Knox W. W. J.** (eds.) *The New Penguin History of Scotland*, Penguin, London, 2001.

Hume Brown, P., *Story of a Nation: Scotland*, Lang Syne Publishers Ltd., Glasgow, 1990.

Hunter, James, *A Dance Called America*, Mainstream Publishing, Edinburgh, 1994.

James, Alwyn, *Scottish Roots*, Luath Press, Edinburgh, 2002.

Katcher, Philip, *The American Civil War*, Brassey's, London, 2003.

Lynch, Michael, *Scotland, a New History*, Pimlico, London, 2001.

MacCulloch, Donald B., *Romantic Lochaber, Arisaig and Morar*, Lines Publishing, Spean Bridge, 1996.

MacDonald, Charles, *Moidart Among The Clanranalds*, Birlinn, Edinburgh, 1997.

Macdonald, Donald J., *CLAN DONALD*, Macdonald Publishers, Loanhead, 1978.

MacDonald, Norman H., *The Clan Ranald Of Lochaber*, no publisher quoted.

Macfarlane, Margaret and **Alastair**, *The Scottish Radicals*, Spa Books, 1981.

MacKay, DR. James, *Pocket History of Scotland*, Parragon, Bath, 2002.

MacKinnon, Charles, *Scottish Highlanders*, Barnes and Noble, New York, 1984.

MacLean, Fitzroy, *A Concise History, Scotland*, Thames and Hudson, London, 2001.

MacLeod, John, *Highlanders*, Sceptre, London, 1997.

Mackie, J. D., *A History of Scotland*, Penguin, London, 1964.

MacNie, Alan, *Clan MacDonald*, Cascade Publishing Company, Jedburgh, 1989.

Magnusson, Magnus, *Scotland: The Story of a Nation*, Harper Collins, London, 2000.

Mills, Hazel, *Scottish Quotations*, Harper Collins Publishers, Glasgow, 1999.

Moffat, William, *A History of Scotland, 1, 2 and 3*, Oxford University Press, Oxford, 1985.

Pearson, Heasketh, *Johnson and Boswell*, Cassell Publishers, London, 1958.

Pittock, Murray G. H., *A New History of Scotland*, Sutton Publishing, London, 2003.

Prebble, John, *Culloden*, Penguin, London, 1961.

Prebble, John, *The Highland Clearances*, Penguin, London, 1969.

Ray, Celeste, *Highland Heritage*, University of N. Carolina Press, 2001.

Scottish Office Agriculture & Fisheries Department, emigration files: ex AF51/17.

Smout, T.C., *A Century Of The Scottish People 1830-1950*, Fontana Press, London, 1997.

Smout, T.C., *A History of The Scottish People 1560-1830*, Fontana Press, London, 1997.

Smout, T.C. and **Wood, Sydney**, *Scottish Voices 1745-1960*, Fontana Press, London, 1991.

Scott, Tom, *Tales of Sir William Wallace*, Gordon Wright Publishing, Edinburgh, 1997.

Scott, Tom, *Tales of King Robert The Bruce*, Gordon Wright Publishing, Edinburgh, 1969.

Steel, Tom, *Scotland's Story*, Collins, Glasgow, 1984.

Stone, Norman (ed.), *The Times Atlas of World History*, Guild Publishing, London, 1989.

Thomson, Derrick S. (ed.), *The Companion to Gaelic Scotland*, Gairm Publications, Glasgow, 1994.

Tranter, Nigel, *The Story of Scotland*, Neil Wilson Publishing, Glasgow, 2003.

Tranter, Nigel, *The North East*, Hodder and Stoughton, London, 1974.

Watson, Fiona, *Scotland, A History 8000 B.C – A.D 2000*, Tempus, London, 2002.

Yeoman, Peter, *Medieval Scotland*, Batsford Books, London, 1995.

Youngson, A. J., *The Prince and the Pretender*, Mercat Press, Edinburgh, 1996.